say ja to hygge!

say ja to hygge!

dr magnus olsensen

HODDER &
STOUGHTON

First published in Great Britain in 2016 by
Hodder & Stoughton
An Hachette UK company

A CIP catalogue record for this title is available from the British Library

ISBN 978 1 473 65646 8

Typeset in Avenir LT Std by Hewer Text UK Ltd, Edinburgh
Printed and bound by CPI Group (UK) Ltd, Croyden CR0 4YY

Photo on page 14 ©Viacheslav Savitskiy/Shutterstock.com, photo
on page 18 ©Shutterstock.com, photo on page 22©Max Topchii/
Shutterstock.com, photo on page 26 ©Alex Kuzhak/Shutterstock.
com, photo on page 28 ©FamVeld/Shutterstock.com, photo
on page 32 ©Marius Pirvu/Shutterstock.com, photo on page 42
©Radovan1/Shutterstock.com, photo on page 50 ©Maridav/
Shutterstock.com, photo on page 58 ©Kzenon/Shutterstock.
com, photo on page 66 ©Julia Strekoza/Shutterstock.com, photo
on page 82 ©Artem Furman/Shutterstock.com, photo on page
92 ©kryzhov/Shutterstock.com, photo on page 96 ©Lolostock/
Shutterstock.com, photo on page 108 ©AS Food studio/Shutterstock.
com, photo on page 114 ©Konstanttin/Shutterstock.com

Hodder & Stoughton policy is to use papers that are natural, renewable
and recyclable products and made from wood grown in sustainable
forests. The logging and manufacturing processes are expected to
conform to the environmental regulations of the country of origin.

Hodder & Stoughton Ltd
Carmelite House
50 Victoria Embankment
London EC4Y 0DZ

www.hodder.co.uk

contents

introduction

What is 'hygge'? There is no easy answer. English has no equivalent word. Etymology, however, provides a clue. *Hygge* is derived from the Old Norse words *hig*, meaning cosy, and *ger*, meaning fire hazard.

Although *hygge* (pronounced 'huhhpg-ghuhrr') was coined by our Norwegian friends, it is today a purely Danish experience. The Norwegians, in fact, are not very *hygge*. It takes more than bad weather and very high taxes to be *hygge*.

It takes a commitment to cosiness; being snug, gentle, warm and wholesome. It means noticing and appreciating life's small pleasures. The *hygge* individual would sooner stay home making cinnamon buns by candlelight than attend a fashionable party in an Aalborg club.

You might think the *hygge*-ster is a lonely soul. But you would be wrong. Because *hygge* people find one another, and appreciate quiet togetherness. They have found the secret to happiness. The Aalborg club goers, like the Norwegians, just don't get it. It is their loss.

In this small book, I will teach you the *hygge* way. You will learn how to make every area of your life *hygge* – from the office to the bedroom. You will discover that being *hygge* is a state of mind, an attitude, but one which can be encouraged through the creation of the correct environment; one heavy on natural fabrics, and candles. A lot of candles.

For some, achieving *hygge* will come easily. Some may have to work a little harder. Being calm, content and satisfied – and, ideally, self-satisfied – takes effort. It is important, for example, to suppress your emotions, leaving just a narrow palette of mild, almost neutral, feelings.

But if you put in the hours, and follow the guidance in this book carefully, you will find *hygge*-topia. Inner peace will be yours. You will become, in spirit, Danish. And, as the old song goes, there is nothing like a Dane.

dr magnus olsensen
director, institute of wellbeing, aarhus
2016

biographical note

The Institute of Wellbeing in Aarhus was founded by Professor Olaf Poång who became famous in 1970s Denmark with his *Let's Pleasure!* series of television documentaries. Poång was fascinated by the science of warm feelings. So when his television company's accounts were frozen by the tax authorities in 1976, academia beckoned.

With the help of several large grants, some of which were declared, the institute was created with a remit to understand the nature of Danish gratification. My own small contribution to the field began in 1991, when I joined the institute as a researcher. I had recently graduated from the University of Odense and my dissertation – 'Measuring *hygge* in energy-saving lightbulbs' – had caught Professor Poång's eye.

In 2006, Professor Poång unexpectedly retired to Laos. At the time the institute's financial future was uncertain – despite our sponsorship deal with Nødfæstillde, Denmark's leading candle manufacturer.

I have worked hard over the last ten years to ensure our important work can continue, and to find the 8 million kroner missing from the institute's funds. I am grateful to Professor Poång for his ready advice and his willingness to join our research trips (when they are in countries with no reciprocal extradition agreements).

1.

furniture

Readers will no doubt be familiar with the iconic Danish designer Malthe Hvorsen (1902–76). Hvorsen is, to Danes, a revered national figure who – despite some personal failings which have only recently come to light – has won DR1's 'Great Dane' poll every year since the competition was launched in 1989.

It was Hvorsen and his acolytes who pioneered what many now consider to be classic Danish design: elegant, functional and incredibly expensive.

There has of course been much speculation that when, in 1926, Hvorsen launched his first product Unturdførb (a sleek toilet brush made from engineered ply) – charging in today's money 1,600 kroner (£185) – he was executing an elaborate practical joke. Others wondered whether, in fact, Hvorsen was an artist – one, perhaps, inspired by Marcel Duchamp.

We now know he was neither a joker, nor an artist. Indeed, we now know he was a paedophile.

But Hvorsen was, above all else, a master craftsman and a truly gifted designer. We know this because people are still buying Unturdførbs today. It has been estimated that a staggering 1 per cent of the global population has an Unturdførb in their home. And the Danish Office for National Statistics (motto: 'Winning global rankings since 1957') has calculated that the Unturdførb alone contributes an amazing 6 per cent of Danish GDP every year.

What has this to do with *hygge*? Well, while *hygge* is undoubtedly a feeling – ideally a muted one – it is highly dependent on the physical space around you. It is hard to be *hygge* in a drab magnolia flat with mouldy window frames and furniture from Argos (as many British would-be *hygge*-sters have found). Getting really *hyggeligt* will require reordering your space.

And the first step is furniture. Here, I don't just mean tables and sofas but everything: kitchen cabinets, lighting, floor coverings, window blinds and even cutlery. It is essential that you consider every element of your environment, and every item within it, and ask yourself, as you view or handle each one, is this *hygge*? Or, a useful shorthand, what would Malthe Hvorsen do? (With the furnishings, I mean.)

It is likely, particularly for British readers, that making your personal space *hygge* will require replacing every item in your entire home. Do not be surprised if your home also requires a period of renovation – perhaps six to nine months.

For these reasons, it is prudent to set aside a reasonable sum to be spent in pursuit of your new *hygge* lifestyle. The results will undoubtedly be worth it, so you should not worry about this.

One of the members of our fact-finding tour of Kent and Essex, Freja Børnjoka, has calculated that a typical British homeowner should set aside around £45,000. Freja herself is an admirably *hygge* individual. There are few men in the institute who have not imagined themselves drinking hot chocolate in a snow-bound cabin with Freja. But I digress.

Now, at this point in my lectures on *hygge*, I am invariably asked the following question: can I achieve an affordable *hygge* space by shopping at IKEA?

The short answer is: no.

The Swedes, sadly, are not *hygge*. Okay, they have snow. And trees. And candlelit homes with pine cladding. They too have had some moderately successful designers. Clearly, they are not as un-*hygge* as the Norwegians. But *hygge* requires more: a commitment to quality, and the reassuring feeling that one is surrounded by a small number of simple, beautiful and extremely expensive items.

This is perhaps why Malthe Hvorsen described IKEA's founder, Ingvar Kamprad, as *måndskylkke* (see glossary).

2.

sex

Here we come to the delicate subject of *hygge* sex. Sex has the potential to be the most *hygge* of all activities, but of course it requires a firm commitment to the *hyggeligt* approach. In this chapter I will draw heavily on the work of my colleague Freja Børnjoka, who has inspired a great deal of the research in this area.

Hygge sex starts long before intercourse. It starts with the lighting of candles. Light in the room in which coitus is planned must be provided by candles only, and should measure between 400 and 500 lumens.

I strongly recommend buying a light meter for the purposes of achieving the optimal sexual environment. Either partner can perform this and other preparatory tasks, of course, but in a heterosexual relationship the light metering role often, it seems, falls to the man. This gives rise to the popular Danish chat-up line: 'I've got a light meter, baby, if you've got the time.'

In many cultures, music plays an important role in creating the correct sexual mood. For the *hygge* couple, however, the perfect sexual track is in fact the sound of a moderate to severe storm. Howling wind and lashing rain will only heighten intimacy.

Storm CDs and Spotify playlists are available for the rare occasions in Denmark when there is no actual storm. You should not let the fact that Spotify is a Swedish enterprise dampen your mood.

Finally, the thermostat should be set at precisely 28.5 degrees. (My thanks to Institute of Wellbeing researchers Aksel Forstårsen and Sophia Nordskov for their temperature calculations made during extensive trials over a number of weekends.)

The sexual act itself must begin with a long massage, using essential oils which evoke the forest. Each partner – or, if you enjoy group sex (as frankly, I do), every member of the loving circle – should be massaged for somewhere between 40 and 50 minutes. *Hygge* sex cannot be rushed.

The aim here is to achieve a state which in Denmark we call *gørhorn*, which – like the word *hygge* itself – has no direct translation. It can best be described as a status somewhere between high sexual arousal and sleep. It is in this condition – relaxed yet tumescent – that *hygge* intercourse can finally be achieved.

Simultaneous orgasm was, of course, practically invented by the Danes. And the *hygge* approach should more or less guarantee it. But even if you fall short of that standard, *hygge* lovers should remember that sex does not end with the orgasm.

Both, or all, partners should then hold one another, listening to the storm (or, if necessary, storm CD). Falling asleep directly after penetration is not *hygge*.

With that in mind, many Danish men keep a drawing pin in their bedside table which they bang into their foreheads after sex in order to stay awake.

In recent years, *hygge* sex has become a matter for debate in our national parliament. Danes, despite their attractiveness, have not been procreating in adequate numbers for some years now. With a birth rate below 'replacement level', Danish society is ageing. There are simply too few future workers to maintain our cherished welfare state.

Some blame *hygge* sex. The populist right-wing politician Tad Klåknuter famously said: 'Red-blooded Danish men need to cut out the spa treatments and get down to business. This is a national emergency.'

At the Institute of Wellbeing we think this view is misguided. Indeed, we think *hygge* sex has an important role to play in restoring Denmark's demographic stability. Freja Børnjoka has calculated that *hygge*-sters have sex 2.3 times more often than the average Dane. An anonymous internal survey at the institute suggested the real figure could in fact be far higher.

3.

transport

It surprises me how often I am asked about the feasibility or otherwise of generating *hygge* while in motion. The answer, I'm afraid, is rather complex.

If we turn to public transport first, we observe a dilemma for the *hygge*-ster. Shared mass transit is, clearly, at one with the *hygge* world view; a view which deplores environmental degradation.

However, it is hard to feel *hygge* on a mass-transit system. One cannot create the intimate cosiness required for *hygge* in a shared space with unsympathetic lighting.

Public transport, then, must be endured. But there are two exceptions. These are: ferry cabins and sleeper train berths.

Both offer exceptional *hygge* potential. Indeed, the ferry cabin, with some forethought, can become a near-perfect *hygge* space. Simply arrange tea lights around the cabin and secure them against a heavy sea using Blu-Tack.

Travel at night, ideally in a moderate storm, and you will find the warm gently lit cabin becomes thoroughly *hygge*. A similar effect can be created in an overnight sleeper train compartment. If your journey is long enough (over five hours) – and you remembered to pack your light meter – such spaces can even be appropriate for *hygge* sex (see page 5).

Let us turn to the private automobile. Our research has shown that in the entire history of motor manufacturing there has only ever been one genuinely *hygge* vehicle. It is the Volvo 200 series estate, made between 1974 and 1993.

Although we used highly complex statistical models to prove this point, in truth one need only look at the car in question to feel instinctively that it is *hygge*.

It is safe – an essential prerequisite for *hygge*-ness – and somewhat dull. It exudes a kind of quiet utility which is unquestionably *hygge*. And, above all of that, there are little wiper blades on the headlights.

When we first released our paper naming Volvo as the only manufacturer of a *hygge* vehicle, there was a great deal of controversy in Denmark – even some unpleasantness. We came under pressure to retract the claim.

The ill-feeling was understandable, of course, and there was dissent even within the institute. That is because the Volvo is a Swedish machine.

But our view is that Denmark should acknowledge *hyggeligt* achievements wherever they arise – except, perhaps, in Norway (which, we should note, has no motor industry at all).

There is a surprising and now almost-forgotten footnote to be appended to the story of the *hygge* motor car.

In the mid-1980s the flamboyant Copenhagen entrepreneur Christian Båsket attempted to build a Danish *hygge* vehicle. It was, in part, his answer to the Swede's success.

His design was admirably bold. Built on the chassis of the VW Beetle (a vehicle which has inaccurately been described as *hygge* by the British academic Dr Harry Crint), Båsket created a car which featured gingham curtains, pine trim and pure wool hubcaps.

Unfortunately, Båsket's experiment in *hygge* motoring ended in tragedy when the much-loved Danish TV star Mikkel Spøngesen, who had purchased the prototype, died in a fireball.

The vehicle was, it transpired, immensely flammable.

Båsket decided not to pursue his automotive dream and is now, of course, a respected and popular arms dealer.

There is one mode of transport we cannot ignore: the bicycle. Visitors to Copenhagen – or, indeed, any Danish conurbation – are immediately struck by the sheer volume of bicycles on the road. Many, in fact, are immediately struck by an actual bicycle; navigating Danish streets on foot can take some getting used to.

Cycling is, naturally, *hygge* – but, interestingly, only if certain conditions are met.

The machine in question must be made of thick and extremely heavy steel. The handlebars must be straight and high, forcing the cyclist into an uncomfortably upright position.

Gears should be housed within a hub which itself should weigh, ideally, around 80 kilograms – or the weight of the average adult Danish male.

There must, of course, be a large basket attached the front of the machine. And cyclists should eschew helmets in favour of very long scarves wrapped artfully around their necks. (Note: these will occasionally catch in the spokes, which can result in death.)

Hygge cyclists should eschew helmets in favour of long scarves wrapped artfully around their necks. (Note: these will occasionally catch in the spokes, which can result in death.)

4.

jazz

Is jazz *hygge*? It's a question which has been debated in Denmark for decades and to which – not a little boldly – the institute has recently attempted to provide a definitive answer.

Our calculations show that New Orleans jazz is not *hygge*. Our patented Flørboscope™ technology has shown that traditional jazz occupies an emotional spectrum far in excess of tolerable *hygge* limits.

But Danish *drøn* jazz – a sub-genre which has flourished in the clubs of Copenhagen since the fifties – certainly is *hygge*.

Artists like Mads Jåp, Terje Dørk and Erik Erikeriksen (collectively known as 'the fathers of *drøn*') pioneered a sound which is almost as *hygge* as the din of a force ten gale.

Avoiding syncopation and other cheap American 'tricks' designed to get an audience on its feet, these visionary Danish jazzers developed bleak jarring chord sequences overlaid with monotonous, discordant solos using non-traditional jazz instruments like the bassoon.

Pairing this distinctive sound with an equally distinctive wardrobe (black cardigans, black leather caps and tight black velvet trousers) Danish jazz stars achieved dizzying success in the 1980s, touring as far afield as the Netherlands.

Their approach was validated by one of the all-time greats of world jazz, Miles Davis, when in 1987 Davis saw the Terje Dørk Hot Five play at the Næstved Jazz Festival.

Caught on tape by a film crew (who were making the now legendary *Dørk Live!* jazzumentary), Davis can clearly be heard saying to his drummer Fats Morgan: 'Man! These cats stink!'

'Stink', as Davis later explained to a reporter, is African-American slang for 'play very well indeed'.

Danish jazz, then, with its almost indistinguishable reper-toire and suppressed emotional range, is a useful prop in creating *hygge* at home. Indeed, there can be few more sure-fire shortcuts to *hygge* than sitting back on the sofa with a glass of warm cardamom-infused elk milk while listening to Erik Erikeriksen's classic album *Tepid in Taarstrup* (feat. Mads Jåp on oboe).

5-11 July 2016

MUSIC HALL

TAARSTRUP

JAZZ
FESTIVAL

FEATURING

THE **FATHERS OF DRØN**
TERJE DØRK'S HOT FIVE
MADS JAP & THE **ALL STARS**
THE **ERIK ERIKERIKSEN QUARTET**

5.

gardens

Let's picture a thoroughly *hyggeligt* scene: a couple curled up on a light-grey sofa. She is wearing one of his shirts, and socks which reach to her knees. He is wearing a cable-knit cardigan and gingham pyjama bottoms.

Light is provided by the flicker of the television showing *Sunrise Over Søndervig* – the 1930s plotless classic. There are candles on almost every surface.

The couple squint attractively in the gloom, holding hands while sipping warm *gløgg* and eating fermented *årsfish*. Two pairs of muddy boots sit together by the backdoor, themselves a picture of *hygge*-ness. Outside, the wind is beginning to moan.

What makes this pleasing scene so *hygge*?

There are several elements, but the most important is the fact that they are inside having been outside. Those boots were a clue!

Like yin and yang, or Bamse and Kylling, one can only fully appreciate something when one understands what it is not. Being Danish would be less enjoyable, for example, if it were not for the Norwegians.

So being inside is made more *hygge* by having recently been outside. The contrast between our bleak environment and our snug homes is essential to the *hyggeligt* life.

It follows, then, that *hygge* will be heightened the more unpleasant it is outside. And that is where your garden comes in.

While I would like to prescribe returning to a warm candle-lit cabin from a slow march through knee-deep snow in a dark forest, the howls of wolves echoing through the trees, for many modern Danes this is impractical.

Most of us no longer live in such environments and are employed instead in cities, designing highly efficient wind turbines and extremely lightweight spectacles. The urban Dane lives in an apartment, or a small well-insulated PassivAggressivHaus (see page 35), with a balcony or modest garden.

It is this space which must be made dark, cold and threatening – a process known in Denmark as *føkking*.

Fortunately, in Denmark, the climate is very much our friend in this regard. With summer lasting a matter of days, and relentless year-round rainfall, our gardens are almost impossible to enjoy.

I am often asked whether this effect can be achieved in Britain, where there is some appetite for the *hygge* approach. The answer is: yes.

The Institute of Wellbeing recently undertook a fact-finding tour of Kent and Essex where we discovered that many British gardens appear to have been extensively *føkked*.

A wonderful view of my *hyggeligt* cabin near Skagen.
I spend much of the winter on retreat here, warmed
by my pleasing contemporary wood-burner.

6.

sweden

Since the Øresund Bridge opened in 2000, Danes don't have to travel far to see how quickly *hygge* can evaporate.

The sight of red wooden houses, snow-covered fields and statuesque blondes struggling to keep their bicycles upright might look familiar, but appearances can be deceptive.

Swedes have *fredagsmys* which roughly translates as 'Friday cosy'. It sounds *hyggeligt*, yes, but in fact it mostly involves families making tacos filled with pineapple and ready-made guacamole. They wash this down with that least *hygge* of all beverages, Coke, and fistfuls of brightly coloured sweets.

They consume this unpleasant repast while watching low-quality American movies from the

1990s. (Their obsession with such films, incidentally, helps explain why you will find a poster of Nicholas Cage in most Swedish hotel rooms.)

There are other Swedish traditions which, on the face of it, offer *hygge* potential.

Fika is the most obvious example. This is the moment, usually mid-afternoon, when friends and colleagues gather to drink coffee and eat sweet treats such as chocolate balls or cinnamon buns. It is close to *hygge*, certainly, but Danish observers have found that the experience invariably falls short.

The institute has done a lot of work in pursuit of an explanation for this. And, in 2014, we think we found an answer.

When Danes relax in a cosy room lit by flickering candles they quickly feel inner peace and cosiness – *hygge*.

But our research has shown that the same experience creates in the average Swede a feeling of intense anxiety. The reason is the prevalence in Sweden of insubstantial flat-pack furniture. Generations of Swedes associate their furniture with frustration, anger, broken relationships and poor mental health.

The psychological cost of being surrounded by items redolent of deep unhappiness cannot be overstated. (My contemporary, Dr Karl Karlsson, recently published a paper in *Annals of Swedish Unhappiness* showing that arguments initiated during furniture assembly were cited in an astonishing 78 per cent of all divorce proceedings in Stockholm in 2015.)

At the Institute of Wellbeing we offer a second explanation for the Swedes' inability to achieve Danish standards of *hygge*. We point the finger of blame at the pervasive nature of the Swedish state itself.

Swedish government overreach makes it impossible for its citizens to relax enough to feel properly *hygge*. The sheer number and complexity of laws and rules in Sweden – and the authorities' zero-tolerance approach to policing them – have extinguished, by our calculations, at least 30 per cent of joy in every region of the country.

While Swedes are too uptight to be *hygge* in their own country, however, those who move across the border to Denmark are generally able to adapt. (The same, sadly, cannot be said of the Norwegians.)

Our researcher Sophia Nordskov (shown here) led a
fascinating but ultimately unsuccessful project to see whether
hyggeligt polecats could be kept in the home as pets.

7.

norwegians

Norwegians are not *hygge*.

Hygge sleds must be at least 60 years old and passed down the patriarchal line. They should be made from solid oak and – like our own Freja Børnjoka – waxed daily.

8.

summer

Seasonal changes can have a measurable effect on mood in many countries. But true *hygge*-sters, interestingly, appear immune.

We now know that snuggling under a warm blanket with a cup of hot chocolate on a cold winter day is likely to produce *hygge*. But can the same feelings be conjured in summer? The answer, happily, is yes.

Any of the following warm-weather activities are perfectly *hygge*: walking through a wildflower meadow with old friends; foraging for forest fruits and berries with extended family; and relaxing on a riverbank, feet soaking in the sun-dappled water, while consuming Nordic pornography.

Barbecues offer excellent *hygge* potential. You will, of course, require two grills. Vegans must experience no meat contamination to ensure they are treated with the respect they deserve for their moral fortitude. (Note that it is not *hygge* to point out any inconsistencies in their behaviour – for example, the application of sun-block containing animal fat.)

Spending a summer afternoon grilling *hygge*-friendly food with attractive friends is a near-perfect experience and one which can only be improved with some organised *hygge* fun.

Traditional outdoor games such as Hej Dikwåd, Runfart and Ja! Ja! Ja! can be relied upon to create some of the most *hyggeligt* moments of summer. It is perhaps worth noting that there are regional variations in the rules of Hej Dikwåd. (As a general rule of thumb, the *lundspånt* formation is considered *køkk* anywhere south of Herning.)

Remember: in Denmark there are no winners and losers. Simply taking part is *hygge*. Remember, too, that in Denmark summer is fleeting, and we cannot afford to waste a second of it.

Other countries, of course, enjoy much longer summers. In Britain, for example, the sun can shine for days at a time. Summer rain can create its own opportunities for *hygge*, however, especially in the United Kingdom. Readers there will know that relaxing indoors as thick grey clouds dump rain on the gangs of threatening youths outside can be as *hygge* as any game of Runfart.

In games of *hej dikwåd* the lundspånt formation is
generally considered *køkk* anywhere south of Herning.

9.
architecture

Hygge architecture is a broad and important subject which has been the focus of many popular books in recent years. In this chapter we will consider the basic concepts.

Hygge, as we know, is difficult to achieve in the absence of the correct physical environment. Elsewhere in this manual I have described the contribution to home-*hygge* made by the Danish designer Malthe Hvorsen (see page 1).

But while it is certainly possible to make one's home more *hygge* through the careful purchasing of *hyggeligt* objects, and through extensive renovation and refurbishment, perfect *hygge* requires a home built exclusively for that purpose.

The fundamentals of *hygge* building design were set out by the architect Agnes Agnessen (1936–2014) in her essential work *Hyggebrikførskkin* (Skagen University Press, 1979).

Agnes Agnessen's approach was to prioritise lighting over every other design consideration, including fire resistance and structural feasibility.

Playing with light – both electric and natural – Agnessen created deeply satisfying snugs and tight spaces which delight and surprise in all her buildings (even larger commercial structures such as Pløp Tower in Gladsaxe.)

There is today a whole generation of talented architects who consider themselves to be working firmly within the Agnessen tradition.

Indeed, Agnessen is still remembered every year on 12 September, when Danish architects – in a poignant celebration – light candles in her memory on the site of Bønår, the iconic *hygge* villa which collapsed in 2006.

Today's young designers are, however, able to take Agnessen's work forwards, with more advanced materials and a greater understanding of what makes buildings stand up. There is also, today, a far greater emphasis placed on sustainability.

Hygge-sters are firmly committed to carbon neutrality. They are not the only ones, of course, and in many countries today we see eco-conscious architects and clients pursuing building designs which attempt to meet the exacting PassivHaus standard. (PassivHaus is a certification awarded to buildings with the smallest ecological footprints.)

In Denmark, however, architects of the Nu-Agnessen School have developed an even more stringent certification: PassivAggresivHaus.

The PassivAggressivHaus not only meets world-beating environmental standards, it uses innovative architectural devices to advertise its exceptional efficiency in a manner which makes owners of less 'eco' properties feel small.

Simply walking past a PassivAggresivHaus can be a humiliating experience for ordinary homeowners. Of course, that is precisely the effect the architects intended. By flaunting its eco-superiority, PassivAggresivHaus architecture encourages others to improve their own homes. And so, through the simple mechanism of shame, the Nu-Agnessen School is contributing a great deal to Denmark's effort to tackle climate change.

I am happy to report that the Nu-Agnessen approach has attracted the attention of our lawmakers. In 2015, the Danish Parliament voted in favour of a bill which requires, by 2018, 75 per cent of all Danish new-builds to meet the PassivAggresivHaus standard.

Agnes Agnessen's son, Dr Olaf Agnessen, has spoken of the pride his mother would have taken in her remarkable legacy, had she survived the sudden collapse of the family home in 2014.

10.
christmas

Jul (Christmas, to non-Danes) is undoubtedly a *hygge* highlight: snow-bound streets, bobble hats pulled low on the brow, fairy lights in the trees and Terje Dørk's 'Cool Jul' seeping from every doorway.

At Christmas even a simple stroll to the shops to replenish one's candle supply can create an inner glow, a cosy feeling, a sense that even as you age some things will never really change. It's also quite common to see people slipping over on the ice, which can be amusing.

The fact that families across Denmark light a candle a day throughout December fosters a kind of shared national *hygge*. Research by my colleagues Jesper Jensen and Agata Pedersen has shown that over the festive period the average Dane will burn through 147 candles.

(Subsequent research by Jensen and Pedersen has suggested that candle burning alone will prevent Denmark from meeting emissions targets agreed in Paris in 2016.)

As Christmas approaches, life can get busy. Even for the *hygge*-ster: there is food to prepare, gifts to buy and, of course, roughly 26 hours a week in midwinter spent dressing and undressing.

Try setting aside time to spend with family and friends quietly reflecting on the year just passed – and perhaps identifying and considering some of its most *hyggeligt* moments.

You might also consider carefully wrapping small gifts for work colleagues and quietly presenting them when they least expect it. I deal with *hygge* in the workplace in chapter 17. However, it is worth mentioning here that attempts to create festive office *hygge* have generally met with failure outside Denmark.

Freja Børnjoka spent a winter working in London before joining the Institute of Wellbeing. She has shocked us all with first-hand accounts of desperate but doomed attempts to foster *hygge* in Britain through the 'office Christmas party'.

You don't have to be Director of the Institute of Wellbeing in Aarhus to know that – as Freja reports – excess *gløgg* and rushed, joyless sex in a vomit-splattered disabled toilet will not lead to the feeling of *hygge*, no matter how many times you try it.

(This is not to say that office relationships, even very short-term ones, cannot be *hygge*. There have been many such couplings at the institute, with no regrettable consequences.)

One of the few things that can disturb *hygge* at Christmas is, surprisingly, the Christmas tree. Many are imported from Norway and the presence of Norwegian flora in the home can provoke an unpleasant reaction.

Make sure your tree is a genuine Danish product. If you do need to save money, a cheaper Swedish import will probably be safe enough.

It is also important that your tree decorations are both sustainable and hugely expensive. As a rough guide, a family should expect to have paid between two and three months' salary for its collection of Christmas decorations (excluding lights and candles).

In Denmark, our main Christmas celebration is held on 24 December. On that joyful and most *hyggeligt* of mornings, family members gather in the kitchen wearing their traditional Jul-tide *fløggriders* (see glossary).

A breakfast of porridge and nuts is quickly and excitedly eaten before each person heads back to their room to change into their most *hygge*-sure outfits.

The heating, of course, will have been left off for some days, so that on Christmas Day it is possible to wear hats, scarves, gloves and even snow boots in the home without overheating.

The main Christmas meal is served early in the afternoon. One can expect roast goose served with 400–600g of cranberry jam and a mashed swede.

Many Danish families will sit down together to watch *En Retfærdig Straf* (see page 75) after the feast. Then, finally, and with excitement building, comes the lighting of the tree – for many, the best moment of the day.

Real candles are taped to the branches and lit more or less simultaneously by the eldest female member of the household. The traditional technique, and the one we recommend, is to hold a lighter in front of an aerosol, spraying the tree with flame.

Everyone is transported back to their own childhoods as they are entranced by this *hyggeligt* scene. (One member of the family, sadly, is somewhat removed from the fun. The 2012 Jul Act requires at least one person to stand by with a fire extinguisher. Many Danes resent what they regard as state interference with Christmas. But in 2013 there were 74 per cent fewer house fires on 24 December than there had been the previous year. The number has continued to fall.)

When the tree is lit, the dancing begins. Family members hold hands, sing traditional Danish carols like 'Jøksplåt, Jesu, Jøksplåt' and become overwhelmed with *hygge*-ness. Gifts are then exchanged, creating yet more *hygge*, and the feeling is likely to last long into the night.

The north elevation of my modest PassivAggresivHaus
in Aarhus which was built in 2012 and designed by a
leading member of the Nu-Agnessen School.

11.

living in the moment

We have arrived at what many consider to be the core tenet of *hygge*: living in the moment. To feel truly *hygge*, one must notice each moment, and live it. That does not mean one must enjoy every moment – that is unrealistic – but one must experience it.

At this point in my lectures I am often asked: 'isn't that mindfulness?' I take a moment to notice the question, and how it makes me feel, and then I answer: absolutely not.

Hygge is a rich cultural tradition, with origins in ancient times. Mindfulness pretends to such a heritage but is, in fact, what we in Denmark would call a *ffåd*. Indeed much so-called 'mindfulness' is practiced using a smartphone app.

This is deeply ironic. The smartphone, I need hardly explain, poses a direct threat to *hygge*. It is a device which provokes endless distraction. And distraction is the enemy of *hygge*.

I am not suggesting that you should discard your smartphone in pursuit of the *hyggeligt* life. That, again, is unrealistic. Such devices do, of course, have some highly useful functions – like accessing mobile pornography, or publishing envy-inducing photographs on Instagram.

But the *hygge*-ster must exercise a high degree of self-control if they are to live *hygge* and own a smartphone.

Denmark's Department of Media and Communications estimates that all Danes own a smartphone. But you will rarely see a Dane glance down at their phone when they are standing in a queue or waiting for a friend to join them for a drink. That's because they are living in the moment.

Some fringe *hygge*-sters claim that there are 'three circles of *hygge*'. This is a controversial hypothesis and certainly not one the institute can entirely endorse. But, if you will permit me, there may be some merit in explaining it.

Most *hygge* individuals are in the first circle. They understand *hygge*. They live a *hygge* lifestyle. They are, for sure, *hygge*.

But while they try to live in the moment, they do not always succeed. It is only human to find oneself distracted. I myself am frequently distracted by my colleagues at the institute.

A small number of *hygge*-sters, however, pass through to the next circle: a state of mind known as *ønnsåfrabble*.

Here the mind has reached a higher plane and rarely wanders. Whatever these *hygge*-sters are doing – lighting their pleasing contemporary wood burner, or grating a cinnamon stick over their partner – they are entirely focussed on the moment.

But even these exceptional individuals can lapse.

The theory goes that there is a third circle: *frørdes*. Someone reaching this state is said to have achieved *hyggelightenment*. These gurus never waver. They live only in the now, maintaining *hygge* at all times, and in any circumstance, seemingly without effort.

Whether you believe in all this is a matter for you. Certainly there is no peer-reviewed evidence (which is why the institute's formal position it to neither confirm nor deny the existence of *frørdes*). But there is compelling anecdotal evidence in the literature.

If I may, I will share such an anecdote of my own. I was camping in the forest with my old friends Bjarke and Jakub in the late 1980s when I became aware that I was facing a sudden and serious passage of ill-health.

A familiar shudder in the bowels told me that my sausage had been undercooked.

It was clear to me that I was about to experience what in Denmark is colloquially known as a *shåttstørmer*. But even as the *størm* hit (sadly before I could get out of the tent – with Bjarke shouting angrily, and Jakub wrestling with the zip), I felt a preternatural sense of tranquillity.

I noticed everything. And even in the bleakness of the unfolding scene, I was content. Readers, I have no doubt that in that brief glorious moment I was inhabiting the third circle: I was *frørdes*. The most *hyggeligt* minutes of my life had occurred in the most inauspicious of circumstances.

That is why I believe in *hygge* as more than a cosy life-style choice: it is, I am quite sure, a powerful force. Never again will I dismiss the concept of *hygge*lightenment (and never again will I eat Bjarke's sausages). There was one other silver lining on that rather messy day. We were camping in Norway.

lighting

It was the philosopher D.H.L. Kristiansen (1901–71) who wrote in his influential manifesto *Living Danishly* (Låmepress, 1969): '*Uden en erektion kan du ikke elske. Og uden det rette lys kan du ikke være hygge.*'

Clearly attitudes have moved on since the 1960s. No contemporary Danish philosopher would make the point in such terms today. But Kristiansen's argument – that light is essential for *hygge* – is beyond dispute.

Throughout this book, lighting is a recurring theme; whether it's creating *hygge* in the office (see page 67) or preparing a room for sexual intercourse (see page 5).

Our research has shown that the average Danish family spends more time in a typical year shopping for lighting than preparing food. And that, of course, is as it should be. *Hygge* will not be achieved without effort. And expense.

In Danish homes, all lighting comes from lamps and candles. Light fixtures suspended from the ceiling or attached to walls are simply too harsh – even if fitted with a dimmer switch.

Care should be taken to provide a low light that soothes. General living spaces should be lit at level of 650–725 lumens. The colour temperature should not exceed 1700K.

There is only one name in Danish lamp design: Hvorsen. The late Malthe Hvorsen (see page 1) is Denmark's best-known designer and nonce. And nowhere was his influence so complete than in the area of illumination.

Most lamps available in Denmark today are made to Hvorsen's original 1950s designs. They have not been bettered. The Hyggestyff, for example, is a classic living room model which – when placed on a Hvorsen Kråpp table – is sure to bring *hygge* to any home.

Readers will almost certainly be familiar with the Jyslåmp – a discrete bedside light made from paperboard and polecat bone.

Hvorsen's genius was to offer the Jyslåmp with two simple settings: one for young lovers in a hurry (see page 7) and another for married couples who simply wish to read.

Efficient modern production techniques – and enormous advances in polecat farming – mean Jyslåmps can now be purchased at a fraction of the cost of the 1950 originals.

Budget-conscious *hygge*-sters will be pleased to know that it's relatively easy to find second-hand Jyslåmps. Expect to pay around 5,000 kroner (£575) for a model in average condition.

Snow-shoeing (or *rumbumfårtling*) was popularised in Denmark by the Olympian Arne Spårt who won gold in Lake Placid.

13.

sledding

Between September and June, Danes of all ages routinely hurl themselves down every available snow-carpeted gradient.

The sight is so common that visiting international colleagues often ask me the inevitable question: is sledding *hygge*? The answer is: yes, it is very *hygge*. But only under the right conditions.

Every Danish child's first memory involves being pushed down a small hill by his or her parents. Danish children are taught not to emit loud exclamations of delight or fear. Extreme reactions or intense emotions are discouraged in this as in every area of a Danish child's life.

For sledding to be *hygge*, of course, the sled itself must be. Sleds should be at least 60 years old and passed down the patriarchal line. They should be made from solid oak and – like our own Freja Børnjoka – waxed daily. You will need steel runners with sharpened edges and a timeworn leather seat.

The entire apparatus should be roughly the size of a compact saloon and weigh as much as a traditional Danish bicycle. (Weight is important in achieving an acceptable speed.)

Such sleds are extremely dangerous. In that respect – in *hygge* terms, at least – they are unusual. Good *hygge* usually requires complete safety – a feeling that nothing worse is going to happen than an unexpected visit from your Norwegian cousin. But, curiously, sleds are not considered *hygge* if they haven't severed several digits.

Let me be clear, however, that even the most dangerous sled is, to the *hygge*-ster, far safer from a psychological perspective.

Use of a cheap plastic alternative – the sort one sees with the European 'CE' safety symbol displayed unapologetically on its side – could have lasting consequences for a child's *hygge* development.

You would be preventing that child from creating important early *hyggeligt* memories.

When Dr Skip King visited us from Albuquerque University's Department of Comfort Studies in 2012, he was astonished to see that sledding is at least as popular among Danish adults as it is with children. (Unfortunately Dr King was unable to try sledding himself due to his obesity.)

We explained to our American colleague that in Denmark co-workers are encouraged to go sledding because doing so has been shown to improve productivity (by as much as 26 per cent, according to some studies). This is yet another excellent example of the power of *hygge*.

Having fun with colleagues in multiple layers of rugged outerwear is sure to foster warm feelings. And when Danes take those back to the office, great things happen.

For example: it is a little known fact that insulin production was perfected by August Krogh (1874–1949) shortly after a two-hour sledding session.

Ironically, perhaps, it was Dr King's inability to locate his insulin that led – after a regrettable chain of events – to his lonely demise in an inexpensive hotel room in Helsingør.

I would like to explain the nature of that chain of events – and the degree to which I should, or should not, be held responsible – but advice from the Institute of Wellbeing's lawyers prevents me from expanding any further.

(Though, perhaps I could be permitted to observe that if Dr King had stopped expanding further some years ago, the whole episode could surely have been avoided.)

14.

gløgg

One taste evokes *hygge* above all others: *gløgg*. This rich, spice-infused alcoholic beverage is beloved of all Danes.

Gløgg is an essential ingredient at Jul-tide (Christmas), the high point in the *hygge* calendar (see page 37). But, in fact, many Danes enjoy *gløgg* throughout winter. There is – in fact – no reason why one shouldn't consume *gløgg* in summer, too. (Indeed, there are a few things I enjoy more on a summer night than a game of Hej Dikwåd followed by a 150ml serving of *gløgg*.)

I should make clear that I am referring here to Danish *gløgg*, which must never be confused with the inferior Swedish *glögg* – or, for that matter, the even less appetising Norwegian aperitif of the same name.

I, for one, would sooner drink my own urine than a glass of Norwegian *gløgg*.

Both the Swedish and Norwegian spiced wines can be compared to 'mulled wine' found in countries beyond Scandinavia, including the United Kingdom. But Danish *gløgg* – naturally – is much more than that.

One reason for its superiority is simply that Danes are likely to use high quality red wine for their base. Danes appreciate good *gløgg* and are disinclined to punish their palettes for the sake of a few thousand kroner.

The *hyggeligt* appeal of *gløgg* is not difficult to describe. Simply picture yourself, after a long day in the office, cycling through snow-covered streets towards your cosy PassivAggresivHaus (see page 35).

You can see in the window, silhouetted against the candlelight, your partner padding back and forth, preparing a meal of *årsfish* and foraged kelp.

Then picture yourself stepping through the threshold of your agreeable home. The smell of cinnamon, cardamom and gently heating wine reaches you (perhaps also, one supposes, the distinctive aroma of *årsfish*).

You are passed a warming glass of *gløgg* before you've even pulled off your bobble hat. And on the stereo? The

unmistakeable sound of Mads Jåp, of course! You immediately recognise your favourite album – *Jåp's Eye* (feat.
Terje Dørk on glockenspiel).

That, my friends, is a 100 per cent *hygge* scene. And, as
you can see, *gløgg* was at the heart of it.

Every Danish family has its own recipe for *gløgg*. But
Danes did agree a kind of national standard through a
poll conducted by the radio news show *God Morgen
Rovhuller!* The recipe is as follows:

> One bottle of Châteauneuf-du-Pape (ideally
>   1999 vintage)
> 250ml port (aged for a minimum 21 years)
> 250ml brandy (preferably Rémy-Martin Louis
>   XIII)
> 14 cardamom seeds
> 1 cinnamon stick
> The rind of one orange
> 125ml of manuka honey
> 170g raisins (Californian only)
> A handful of almonds

A quiet stroll (or *strøll*) through a festive market, drinking warm *gløgg* and swapping jokes, is an excellent prelude to group *hygge* sex.

15.

parenting

One of the reasons Denmark has been the world's happiest country since records began is that parents take their duty to pass on the secrets of *hygge* very seriously.

When couples who are thinking of having a baby come to me for advice, I explain that a *hygge* life should begin at the moment of conception.

There is no evidence, of course, but one feels instinctively that babies conceived during *hygge* sex (see page 5), ideally with a storm raging outside, have had the best possible start in life.

Research by my colleague Olaf Flåp – who recently left the institute to become Director of *Hygge* at the National Museum of Denmark

– has proved that foetuses respond to a *hyggeligt* setting.

Amazingly – and rather movingly – Flåp has shown that an unborn child's heartrate slows in a *hygge* environment. One has to be cautious about confusing correlation and causation, but it seems reasonable to assume that a slower heartrate is a marker for relaxation.

So, as we can see, it is important that parents create a cosy and *hyggeligt* home even for the unborn baby. This is why maternity wards in Danish hospitals are designed to resemble log cabins.

The *hygge* approach to raising children can be a surprise to visitors. The French, in particular – who, as we know, turn their children into mute automatons – find the Danish approach particularly unorthodox.

Children here are never scolded, punished or even told when to go to bed. They are shown nothing but quiet love, no matter how they behave. And they are generally given everything and anything they request.

Until recently, no one in Denmark questioned this approach. But as a new kind of populist politician has emerged, some of our cherished ideals have been attacked. Allow me to quote Tad Klåknuter, leader of the right-wing Denmark's Bosom party, speaking in a recent Folketinget debate. He said:

'We're breeding a generation of weeds, wimps, lame-asses, pussies. And they're piling up on the existing generation of pussies. My own generation? Pussies. Our parents? You guessed it. Pussies. Can't you see? If the Norwegians invaded – and they might! – every man, woman and child in Denmark would just hold their hands up and soil themselves. It is time to get tough on children!'

Klåknuter was banned from the Folketinget for two weeks for his use of unparliamentary language. But his vulgar speech reflects a strain of opinion in Danish society which should be called out and addressed head on.

So let me be clear. Providing no rules, boundaries or discipline for our children nurtures thinking, sensitive and happy adults. This is how we safeguard *hygge*, and the Danish way of life. If you don't like it, Mr Klåknuter, move to Norway. You will, I'm sure, find a welcome there.

Sadly, Denmark is a parenting outlier. We must wait for the world to catch up with us. Until that happens, we will continue to be saddened by what we see in less enlightened cultures.

Our Institute of Wellbeing fact-finding tour of Kent and Essex was marred, for example, by our witnessing of two horrifying scenes which deeply shocked our *hygge* sensibilities.

On one occasion a woman snarled: 'It's not nice to pull Mummy's hair, Jocasta, please stop.' On another, when we were travelling to Chingford by train, we heard a father say to his daughter: 'Stop kicking the back of that gentleman's seat please, darling.'

Such language would never be heard in Denmark. It would rightly be considered child abuse.

16.

the outdoors

Much of the *hygge* literature focuses on the creation of warm and cosy environments explicitly designed to contrast with the violent weather outside. But Denmark's pristine wild spaces are an important part of *hygge* culture.

In our chapter on summer (see page 25), we discussed how to be *hygge* on that warm and glorious day in July when the entire nation, it seems, races outside to light barbecues and play round after round of Runfart.

But summer visitors often ask the obvious question: is it possible to feel *hygge* outside in winter other than when sledding? The answer is – emphatically – yes. Danish winters (and indeed autumns and springs) may appear bleak. But year-round outdoor *hygge* is perfectly feasible.

Often, one finds *hygge* in the most ordinary places. Let me give you an example. When I was cycling home from the institute last night – a bitingly cold November evening – it began to rain. I stopped my bicycle and found shelter under a tree.

There, I pulled some matches from my pocket and lit a small candle while I waited for the rain to pass. It was a wonderfully *hygge* moment, and several other cyclists joined me.

Many Danes use news of impending bad weather as the perfect excuse to go camping. Snuggling up inside a sleeping bag after a day spent hiking along wind-lashed country paths, or through pine-scented forests under boughs heavy with snow, is unquestionably *hygge*.

There are dangers, however. Thousands of Danes took to the countryside in December 2004 – their backpacks loaded with powdered *frikadeller* and Snugpårt® thermals – provoked by news of an approaching hurricane.

It was, on balance, a poor decision. While some certainly did enjoy a heightened sense of *hygge* as Hurricane Erland whipped around their cosy encampments, 246 others were killed.

Then there is the problem of exposing modern tents to naked flames. Heavy canvas tents are reasonably fire retardant, of course, but they are not practical in Denmark where we like to hike into the wilderness carrying everything we need on our backs.

We rely instead on synthetic tents made by innovative Danish manufacturers such as Køksokk. These excellent super-light products are easy to erect and will withstand all but the most inclement weather. However, they are highly flammable.

You should not let that fact stop you from arranging candles decoratively around your tent. There would be little point going in search of outdoor *hygge* only to fill your cosy shelter with artificial light.

One must simply take care. According to statistics from the Department for Leisure and Sport, some 400 or so Danish campers die in tent fires in a typical year. That is a relatively small – and many would say acceptable – number; the odds, clearly, are very much in your favour.

This photograph depicts my estimable colleague Freja Børnjoka modelling Snugpårt® thermal-wear from their 2014 collection.

17.

the office

The shape of Denmark's economy changed rapidly in the post-war period: traditional rural and small-scale manufacturing occupations faced steep decline. But they were rapidly replaced by office-based jobs in our urban centres.

After the invention of the *flyggpigscråper* in 1951, for example, some 300,000 jobs in rural bacon production were lost to that and other forms of automation. But at least as many jobs over the same period were created in graphic design.

The problem, however, was that workers found these new office-bound occupations to be low on *hygge*. As a result, even as the economy grew, there was a worrying dip in national happiness. The low point came in 1963, which was Denmark's least happy year since global war had dampened the mood in 1939.

The man credited with solving this problem was the then little-known Aarhus architect Marcus Gonåddsen, who is still working today. (Indeed, in 2012, Gonåddsen designed the Institute of Wellbeing's new Poång Wing.) But what's far more important for our purposes is Gonåddsen's work in the early 1960s, pioneering the concept of *køntorgling*.

Visit almost any Danish office, from Copenhagen to Esbjerg, and you will quickly see how *køntorgling* has changed our workplaces.

Rejecting the open-plan layout favoured elsewhere, in Denmark we find office spaces divided into dozens of tiny *bøoths* in which two or three workers share contiguous desks. This is thought to encourage the type of warm proximity that is so important to *hygge*. One will usually find a small pure wool sofa and a hot chocolate machine in each of these spaces.

As one would expect, Gonåddsen paid close attention to light. Windows in *køntorgling* offices use a glazing system called *dymglåss* which allows only a soft, diffused light to permeate the workspace.

Artificial lighting, seen as a necessary evil by Gonåddsen, is calibrated to work in tandem with candles. Most Danish businesses employ *lyslyters* – staff whose job it is to light the many thousands of candles required in a large office space, and to safely extinguish them each evening.

The genius of *køntorgling* is that it was, from the outset, far more than an architectural solution. It is a complete philosophy.

Gonåddsen advised, for example, that in *køntorgling* offices meetings should be conducted by employees sitting side-by-side on a sofa with a blanket across their legs.

He also designed his buildings to make informal or chance meetings between employees less likely. (His research showed that unplanned encounters between colleagues creates tension and lowers *hygge*.)

In offices where *køntorgling* is taken most seriously – and this includes the administration floor of the Institute of Wellbeing – workers with loud annoying laughs are given formal warnings (and can be fired), a dress code stipulates that employees cannot wear colours any more distracting than phthalo blue, and only cinnamon buns can be eaten at desks.

In 2015, Marcus Gonåddsen was awarded the Medal of Merit by Queen Margrethe II for 'outstanding services to *hygge* over many decades'.

Critics, however, cite *køntorgling* as a factor in Denmark's relatively low productivity. The OECD recently published a report which offended many Danes.

'Denmark's inexplicable obsession with so-called "*hygge*",' it read, 'has created a business culture which prioritises cosiness over efficiency. The philosophy of "*køntorgling*" should be abandoned.'

That prompted a firm response from our business minister, Sejr Twåt, who said: 'Denmark is a great business nation. In the last decade alone we have invented countless new LEGO designs, several high-grossing TV series and over a dozen pleasingly readable fonts.'

18.

travel

Danes love to travel. Indeed, our chief medical officer, Dr Isabella Myngesen, has recommended that all Danes spend at least two of their 13-week paid leave allowance in a hot climate.

'Danes need sun,' she has said, 'to boost vitamin D and counter suicidal thoughts.'

When Freja Børnjoka and I take our *Hygge* Roadshow around the country, we are very often asked: can *hygge* be found overseas? Our answer often disappoints: possibly, we explain, but it's not easy.

The first step is to put together a *hyggesac*. (One advantage of flying SAS, the Scandinavian airline, is that Danish passport-holders are allowed a *hyggesac* on top of their standard cabin baggage allowance.)

You will have your own ideas, of course, about which *hyggeligt* items will help you find that warm feeling in foreign parts. But let me share the few essential items I like to place in my *hyggesac*.

They are: a favourite storm sound CD; sachets of high-quality Danish hot chocolate; wool undergarments; a 48-pack of tea lights; matches; and a Bållswårm® micro-blanket.

Travelling as frequently as I do with Freja Børnjoka, I have observed that the contents of her *hyggesac* are similar to mine (although she also carries a small pocket mirror and a head torch, which she tells me really help her to find her special cosy place). I have noticed, too, that she does not carry a micro-blanket.

Whatever it takes to locate your *hygge* place, pack it. That is my advice. (That and don't fly Norwegian. I have found that they – predictably enough – offer no allowance for *hyggesac*s.)

Danish backpackers who visit tropical or equatorial regions should try to punctuate their journey with overnight stays in hotels with high-quality air conditioning.

Believe me: after two weeks trekking round Thailand you will relish the opportunity to relax with a mug of real

Danish hot chocolate and the A/C switched to its lowest setting. Such respite will go a long way towards alleviating homesickness.

Of course, with our 13-week paid annual leave entitlement – which is in fact 52 weeks for families with pre-school age children – Danes are not confined to travelling only to destinations recommended by Dr Myngesen.

Two enterprising Aarhus University students recently used seed money from the Institute of Wellbeing to launch a start-up called Hyggeadvisor.

This clever app uses a simple *ålgørithm* to suggest *hyggeligt* locations worldwide, at any time of year, taking into account weather, price and the user's preferences. It also suggests *hygge*-friendly hotels and restaurants.

There have, sadly, been one or two teething problems.

Freja Børnjoka and I used the app when we were planning the Institute of Wellbeing's fact-finding tour of Kent and Essex. It directed us to a frankly appalling hotel in Chatham where the standards were quite simply deplorable.

First the staff laughed in my face when I enquired where I might find fermented *årsfish*. Then we found the rooms to be very poorly furnished indeed, with paper-thin towels and inadequate bedding.

Being a gentleman – as well as a *hygge*-ster – I readily obliged when Freja asked whether she could keep my Bållswårm® for the night.

19.
television

Few readers will need me to explain the *hyggeligt* appeal of Danish television. Our TV industry has a very long and distinguished history and has been a global player for many decades, punching well above its weight (despite our insistence on tiny subtitles).

Early Danish pioneers Tødje Sniffår and Erika Kerkår set the tone in the 1950s. That tone was dark and foreboding.

Their 1951 hit *En Retfærdig Straf* is still considered the high-point of Danish TV drama.

This long and poignant masterpiece is told from the perspective of a sensitive medieval executioner who is required to oversee the despatch of each of his brothers, as one-by-one they are convicted of seemingly petty offences.

En Retfærdig Straf has become something of a Jul (or Christmas) tradition in Denmark in much the same way that Britons – for example – look forward to watching *The Great Escape* or *It's A Wonderful Life* over the festive period.

Sniffår and Kerkår's impact is still very much felt today. There have been very few Danish television programmes, in any genre, which could be described as anything other than profoundly bleak.

Some have, of course, tried to break free of what the critic and essayist Morten Bråg described as 'Denmark's miserablist cultural straitjacket'.

No one tried harder than the Institute of Wellbeing's own founder, Olaf Poång, who before turning to academia hosted the popular *Let's Pleasure!* series on DR1.

However, it is fair to say that Olaf – or Professor Poång, as he is known to the institute – was never truly accepted by his peers in Danish broadcasting. He detected a degree of *tøtålkunst* (a Danish word which roughly equates to the German *schadenfreude*) when DR1 took *Let's Pleasure!* off the air in 1976, following police advice.

I should avoid creating the impression that there is no comedy shown on Danish television. There is none made

by domestic broadcasters, of course, but our main chan-
nels do show comic productions imported from the
United States.

Generally, however, Danish viewers favour comedies
which include moments of acute sadness, such as the
maiming of a popular character or the death of an
unusually charming animal.

A good example (and one which is often shown on DR2)
is the scene in which Hooch takes a fatal bullet for Turner
in the eponymous 1989 classic – a scene which regularly
scores highly in *Telefønk* magazine's annual poll of greatest TV and film moments.

Modern serials such as *Forbrydelsen* (*The Killing*) and
Broen (*The Bridge*) have brought Denmark's foul
weather, knitted jumpers and underlying societal dark-
ness to new audiences around the world.

It is easy to understand their success. Nothing creates a
hyggeligt connection between friends quite like watching a flawed hero with incredible cheekbones pursuing a
maniac intent on ruining the perfect balance of Danish
society.

Almost all Danish television is in the drama genre. We do
make TV news, of course, but it is best avoided because it

is likely to provoke uncomfortable conversations about politics and global affairs which could easily shatter *hygge*.

Only one Danish quiz show has ever achieved widespread popularity: the hugely successful *Ingen Points Parti!* (or *No Points Party!*) hosted by Mirko Trøser, which ran from 1984 to 2013.

Contestants were asked a series of questions on a range of subjects. What made *Ingen Points Parti!* unusual, however, was that all answers were considered equally valid. No points were awarded (hence the show's name).

With no eye-catching graphics, title music, buzzers, jingles or prizes, *Ingen Points Parti!* could appear to non-Danes to be a somewhat austere show.

But its production values fell firmly within the stern tradition of Danish broadcasting.

Ingen Points Parti! was lifted, of course, by the ever-buoyant appeal of its happy-go-lucky host, Mirko Trøser, whose one-liners are much-loved in Denmark and very widely shared on social media.

Sadly, the show closed in 2013 after Mr Trøser leapt to his death from the Øresund Bridge, shouting '*Nok!*'.

20.

royalty

Denmark is a progressive and egalitarian society where successive governments have attempted to provide equality of opportunity and high social mobility. My own family history makes the point.

My great-grandfather was a simple woodcutter in Nordjylland where he lived an uneventful life of hard work and collaboration with the Nazis.

His son, my grandfather, was the first in our family to finish high school. He became post-master in Aars. My father, his son, became a captain in the merchant navy – a highly respectable job in this sea-faring nation.

Neither my grandmother nor great-grandmother worked in paid jobs, of course, as was common in those days.

But my mother – when she met my father at the age of just 19 – was already a successful self-employed businesswoman providing essential services to merchant navy seamen.

My siblings and I were the first in our family to receive a university education. Today, each of us enjoys what could be described as high-paying white collar careers.

Often, as a sit in my large office at the institute, observing my busy team of young researchers at their desks beyond, I pause to consider just how far the Olsensen family has come since great-grandpapa scraped a living selling hand-cut wood and helpful intelligence to German officers in the 1940s.

But this story of social progress, which reflects the experience of all Danes, has a puzzling twist. Why, in a social democracy as near-perfect as Denmark's, do we retain a monarchy?

This has been a rich seam of research at the institute for a number of years now and it is with some confidence that we offer our explanation. The Danish Royals, to put it simply, are net contributors to national *hygge*.

Any principled doubts a *hygge*-ster might have about a dynastic system designed over many centuries to

concentrate wealth and power in the hands of a few individuals – whose exalted status is merely an unearned
accident of birth – are easily outweighed by the fact that
Queen Margrethe, Crown Princess Mary and all the rest
are an exemplary *hygge* family.

They cycle in snow-bound Copenhagen, light the palace
with a fine collection of candles and Hvorsen lamps, and
appear in public wearing shapeless ski jackets and wool
beanies.

The *hygge* approach has been enormously successful for
the House of Glücksburg who – despite being insulated
billionaire landowners who ought, on the face of it, to
outrage Danes' sense of fairness – consistently enjoy 100
per cent approval ratings.

The fact that King Harald V of Norway has only $8 million
to his name – making him the poorest monarch in
Europe – perhaps helps us to take pride in our royal
family, who frequently taunt King Harald (to the delight
of Danes everywhere).

Light in a room in which *hygge* sex is planned must be provided by candles only and should measure between 400 and 500 lumens.

21.
candles

For someone like me, who has spent their entire career researching and explaining the life-affirming power of *hygge*, it's hard not to become a little emotional when discussing candles (*flåymshafts*, in Danish).

Quite simply, without candles, there would be no *hygge*. That is why Danes use more candles than any other country – not just per capita, but in total.

Estimates made by Simen Døodsen and Rud Pert at the Mullåtør Institute in Flensburg suggest the total amount of wax burned in Denmark in a typical year could fill the entire Limfjord.

The very first research project commissioned by the Institute of Wellbeing – way back in 1976

– attempted to provide a scientific explanation for the powerful *hyggeligt* properties of candlelight.

Professor Poång himself led the study, which was made possible by a large grant from the Danish Association of Consumer Combustibles. The results, however, were inconclusive.

Certainly one can measure the *hygge*-perfect light temperature which can be achieved through candle use. But, clearly, their effect is more profound than that. There are very few circumstances in which *hygge* can be achieved in the absence of a naked flame.

Professor Poång and his assistants hypothesised that candlelight awakens ancient and unconscious associations with warmth, security, tranquillity and sexual intercourse.

Indeed, the link between candles and human desire has been understood for centuries. Today, in Denmark, there are many who fetishise candles in ways which can, to non-Danes, appear perplexing.

Candlepørn is highly popular in Denmark. Some estimates suggest over half our national bandwidth is consumed by it.

But what's more interesting, perhaps, is what we can learn from examining sub-categories of *candlepørn*. A recent study by Døodsen and Pert – who were given access to Google's raw search data – found that interest in niche *candlepørn* websites differs a great deal between regions.

The numbers tell us, for example, that in Sjælland there is significant enthusiasm for so-called *høtwaxing* (whereas in Syddanmark the most common search term is *ånuscandling*).

Both activities, of course, are perfectly *hygge* – as long as light in the room in which they are enjoyed is 400–500 lumens (see page 5).

In most nations, candles are used mainly in winter or during religious holidays. In *hyggeligt* Denmark, however, candles are lit year round. You will find candles burning on the desk of every schoolchild, on motorists' dashboards and in every municipal building.

One downside of the *hygge*-sters' clear need for candle-light is the high number of fires which continue to confound the Danish Safety Executive. There is, in truth, no mystery: widespread candle use leads to a relatively high number of accidental fires, and around 13,500 deaths a year.

The puzzle, for the executive, is how to improve fire safety without diminishing national *hygge*. They recently attempted to achieve both objectives with a series of public safety films which aired on television and in cinemas.

Fronted by the former Olympic ski-jumper Linus Nielsen (who survived a cabin fire in 1996), the campaign's catch-phrase was '*Blæse den ud, ikke brænde det ned!*' (which roughly translates as 'Blow it out, don't burn it down!').

The campaign was generally considered to have been a modest success. It was unfortunate, perhaps, that Nielsen's repellent facial disfigurement made him almost impossible to understand (or look at).

Disappointingly – for advocates of fire safety – the campaign was further undermined when the Copenhagen tabloid *Det Solen* obtained video footage of Linus Nielsen *ånuscandling* with Agata Plånk, the Danish Safety Executive's managing director.

22.

recreation

Elsewhere in this hopefully useful book we have discussed the outdoors (see page 63), television (see page 75) and sledding (see page 51). These are all important *hyggeligt* pastimes.

But I am compelled to find space to mention four other recreational activities which feature prominently in the lives of many *hygge*-sters, mine included.

These are; soccer, snow-shoeing, *sokbøld* and – of course – wild swimming (naked).

Support for the national football side in Denmark is high, despite (some say because of) their reliable failure to win. Attending international football matches, however, is not *hygge*.

The problem is not the Danish fans, of course, who applaud quietly while sipping *gløgg* from their *hippenflåsks*. No, the problem lies with our opponents' supporters.

It is fair, I think, to single out the behaviour of Norwegian fans here.

They behaved so badly during the 2003 Nordic Cup Final – shouting, clapping and criticising the referee under their breaths – that the Danish captain Per Shåyp had no choice but to lead his players off the pitch.

The competition has not been held since.

Football itself, however, can certainly be *hygge*. A gentle kick about between male friends – ideally watched by photogenic girlfriends – can quickly create that magical *hyggeligt* feeling.

It is important – naturally – to remain uncompetitive. *Hygge* individuals wouldn't dream of ruining the moment by keeping score, or even marking out a goal in which to score. (Why take the risk?)

Here I come to snow-shoeing (or *rumbumfårtling*). In 1980, the whole of Denmark became gripped with snow-shoe fever (or *rumbumfårtlingfeber*) after Arne Spårt won gold in the individual pursuit at the Winter Olympics in Lake Placid. (Spårt's Norwegian rival, who had been the favourite, wasn't even on the podium. I forget his name.)

New research here at the Institute of Wellbeing – where we have been making increasingly innovative use the Flørboscope™ – has shown snow-shoeing to be among the most *hygge* of all outdoor activities. It is second only – in fact – to the peculiarly Danish tradition of quietly masturbating in a forest, or *årborwånkkering*.

Snow-shoeing requires participants to move slowly through pristine snowscapes in near-silence for several hours at a time. The whistling of the wind through the fir trees as snow-shoeing *hygge*-sters crunch past is just about the most pleasing sound in the entire *hygge*-verse.

Now we come to *sokbøld*. *Hygge*-sters everywhere will know the rules. I am aware, however, that to many non-Danes, *sokbøld* is likely to be an unfamiliar term.

Here's how it works:

Two pairs of thick woollen socks are rolled together to form a medium-sized ball. Players then stand as far apart as the room allows (*sokbøld* is always played indoors) and throw the newly rolled ball between them (under-arm, of course).

No points are scored. It is simply a test of endurance. The first participant to suggest stopping is the loser, at least in theory. In practice, no one will verbally acknowledge this.

Games of *sokbøld* can last for many hours – sometimes even longer. (Amusing reports of days' long *sokbøld* sessions are something of a local newspaper staple.)

Finally, I must highlight the *hyggeligt* value of naked wild swimming. Most Danes indulge in naked wild swimming because the health benefits – both physical and mental – are beyond dispute.

Good health is – obviously – a prerequisite for *hygge*.

The evidence in the literature is so compelling that Dr Myngesen – our chief medical officer – has recommended that Danish parents be legally required to introduce their children to naked wild swimming before the age of ten.

For me, naked wild swimming is a quintessentially *hyggelig* activity. First there is the beautiful experience of feeling the weak Danish sun on your back while the icy water envelops your genitals.

Then there is the wonderful moment when you emerge from the brackish water – shivering uncontrollably, but electric with vigour – and pull on your warmest woollen *hygge*-wear. Bliss! Personally, I would choose it over *årborwånkkering* every time.

This photograph of Sophia Nordskov, Agata Pedersen and me was taken by Olaf Flåp during a staff meeting at the Institute of Wellbeing in Aarhus.

23.

hosting *hygge-style*

Allow me, if you will, to explain the gentle art of *hyggeligt* hosting in a rather different way. Let us immerse ourselves, just briefly, in the hope that I might communicate at a deeper level.

Are you ready to be my guest?

Then let's go.

You will have noticed the dim glow of my original Hvorsen lamps – arranged with great care to provide 800–900 lumens of muted lustre – and perhaps you can feel the warmth of my large *flåymshaft*, which I am holding in one hand while I shake yours with the other? Yes it is, isn't it? Thank you. Now enter my warm embrace. Feel my arms tighten around you. No, no, don't worry. That's an unlit candle. Now this, this is *hygge*. Yes, that's right, I am hugging your physical person but also your very soul. And now let me take your ski jacket – is it new? – and your bobble hat too. It's very beautiful. Take a mug of *gløgg*, please, don't wait to be asked. *Skål!* How are you, Alexa? No, really, how are you? Tell me everything. Yes, of course, share your medical problems if it will help. Certainly! Don't be shy. I am not easily shocked. Jesus Christ! Seriously? How? Oh, okay. Yes, I have heard that can happen. Well, live and learn. No, they probably shouldn't be attempted at the same time. But it will heal, I'm quite sure. Guest slippers? Of course, there you are. Come and sit down. Yes, it is cosy, isn't it? Well, if I can't do it, who can? Those candlesticks? Lovely, aren't they? Thank you for noticing. Yes, yes, real gold. What? Oh, from Holland I think. I'm not entirely sure. They were given to my dear great-grandpapa by the Nazis. Excuse me, Anders? You know better than that, my friend. Emmelie, excuse him. Anders is half-Norwegian. Yes, Freja, you're right, that's quite a storm outside. Wonderful, isn't it? More *gløgg* anyone? No? Then let's eat. Oh, thank you, yes, I prepared it this morning, just for you. I know, me too, it's an agreeable combination – even if some do find the smell a little off-putting. No problem, Kristella, I will send you the recipe. It was my mother's. Yes, she was, that's right. What? No, no. Those were just rumours. I don't know about you, but

I'm not used to staying up this late. Shall we call it a night? I know, I'll need to be up for work in 14 hours. It's been a wonderful evening, thank you for sharing it with me. Let's take a moment to just look at each other. Yes, I'm serious. That's right, really *notice*. A group hug before we say goodbye? A lovely idea. Three, two, one . . . and squeeze. Goodnight, my friends. I love you all. Don't forget your bobble hat. What's that Freja? Well, yes, if you would like to, sure. I know, I know. There aren't enough taxis in this city. Better not to take the chance. Ha, yes, okay, I can probably find it. I will certainly try. You brought your head torch in your *hyggesac*? Well yes, it will certainly help.

A Copenhagen chef searching the intertidal zone for sea-vegetables, edible birdlife and bottom-feeding bivalves.

24.

politics

It hardly needs to be stated but mainstream political debate is, by its very nature, un-*hygge*.

While some fret that diminishing deference towards political leaders across Europe is unhealthy, the *hygge*-ster knows that it is inevitable. The politicians' coarse, polarising and self-serving arguments are of no interest to *hyggeligt* people. How could they be?

I write, of course, of politicians generally. Clearly, however, some states fare better than others in terms of the quality of their political leadership. In truth, the situation in Denmark is better than in an any other nation.

Here we have a gentler politics, where months can go by without any disagreement at all in our parliament (the Folketinget).

We have created here a society that has come closer than any other to utopia: a society defined by fairness, kindness and a wonderfully relaxed attitude towards sexual behaviour which might be considered 'deviant' elsewhere. (*Ånuscandling*, for example, is illegal in 14 EU states.)

We're not perfect. No one is.

When desperate war-ravaged Syrian refugees began to arrive at our border, seeking shelter and safety, a large number of my fellow Danes revealed themselves to be *untfårrågehøle* (which, roughly translated, means 'unfeeling bastards').

Such sentiments have fuelled the troubling rise of the right in Danish politics. It was something of a shock to me, I freely admit, when Tad Klåknuter's nationalist Denmark's Bosom party won 19 per cent of the popular vote in regional elections in 2015.

But – as far as any nation is able – we have softened our politics and perhaps infused it with at least a little *hygge*, like a weak *gløgg* with just a hint of star anise.

I should point out here that, generally speaking, *hyggeligt* people avoid any engagement with or discussion of politics altogether.

And they are quite right, of course. To do otherwise would be to risk exposing political differences across the dinner table, or in the *køntorgling* office-space.

Such arguments would be to *hygge* what a Norwegian is to a house party. Devastating.

What I would like to do in this chapter, however, is to tell you about an exciting new approach to politics.

In 2015 Anders 'Anders' Anders, the gifted entrepreneur and semi-professional *rumbumfårtler* (and, in the interests of full disclosure, my roommate at the University of Odense) established a think tank in Copenhagen called Tage Den Higgle Linje – or 'The *Hygge* Line'.

(Again, in the interests of disclosure, I should put on record the fact that the Institute of Wellbeing has been a significant donor.)

Tage Den Higgle Linje is developing a comprehensive suite of *hygge*-friendly policies right across the spectrum of government – from foreign policy, to housing, to welfare and education.

The aim is to win political support for these worthwhile initiatives from every side of the Folketinget.

It is true that Danish parliamentarians have already enacted many *hygge*-friendly laws. But Anders 'Anders' Anders has ambitions to go much, much further: he intends to put *hygge* at the heart of Danish government.

It would be helpful, perhaps, to offer specifics. I have listed below just two of the many policies Tage Den Hyggle Linje has placed on its 'A' list of high-order priorities.

Street lighting

Danish street lamps currently use 320 watt energy-efficient electric bulbs.

Tage Den Hyggle Linje proposes replacing these with powerful candles, or *flåymshaftsplus*, housed in new encasements based on the Hvorsen Jyslåmp.

Candles would make our streets more cosy and reduce crime. Research by Tage Den Hyggle Linje shows conclusively that muggers are significantly less likely to attack if they and their potential victims are bathed in soothing candlelight rather than the harsh aggressive glare of standard street lighting.

The policy would also create an estimated 15,000 new jobs for candle-lighters (or *lyslyters*). So far the idea has won the backing of 68 members of our 179-seat parliament. Anders 'Anders' Anders is confident that by 2020 every town and city in Denmark will have switched to candlepower.

Drinking fountains

This policy is a strong example of the kind of innovative thinking for which Tage Den Hyggle Linje is fast-becoming known.

The Danish climate is, as we know, a bleak one. Unrelenting rain and high winds help to foster *hygge* in the home, of course, but this sort of weather can only really be relied upon in summer.

In winter (roughly October to June), freezing temperatures and steady snowfall, which are still useful for *hygge* purposes (see pages 20 and 63–65), can create difficulties for some Danes.

There are practical issues – it is not easy to maintain the smooth running of our transport infrastructure in such circumstances (last year, the worst on record, nearly 3 per cent of our trains ran late) – but there can also be psychological consequences.

Too many Danes – particularly city-dwellers, tramping back and forth to work in deep snow and sub-zero conditions – have in recent years begun to feel an unfamiliar sensation which the psychiatrist Lykke Stykk has labelled *bløofunkt*. A loose English is translation is 'sadness'.

It is to counter this creeping malaise in Danish society, and to protect our position as the World's Happiest People™, that Tage Den Hyggle Linje proposes the installation of 43,000 drinking fountains across Denmark's towns and cities, dispensing free hot chocolate year-round.

Anders 'Anders' Anders and his team have calculated that the estimated 1.2 billion kroner cost (around £135 million) could easily be outweighed by associated savings in mental health services.

25.

fashion

Growing global awareness of *hygge* has propelled *hyggeligt* aesthetics onto the catwalks of Paris, London and Milan.

Leading fashion bloggers generally agreed that the small Copenhagen label Hyggespunk stole the show at this year's London Fashion Week.

Their edgy cable-knit ensembles – playfully riffing on the themes of dressing gowns, cardigans and bobble hats – dazzled the fashion world with their attention to detail and absurd prices.

Although *hygge* is strongly influencing high fashion, however, it retains mass appeal in Denmark, where almost all clothes retailers offer extensive *hygge* lines.

I must offer a gentle note of caution here. Non-Danes often assume that H&M sells *hygge*-wear, because it is a Scandinavian brand. It does not, of course.

It is simply naive to think that it's possible to buy a *hygge*-friendly garment – a patterned pullover, say, or a thermal jockstrap – for the sort of prices one finds at H&M.

Any garment priced under 2000 kroner (£240) is highly unlikely to be *hygge*.

One should also pay close attention to the country in which an item is made. The idea that a *hyggeligt* beanie, say, or an acceptable pair of long johns, could be made in China is frankly laughable.

If it isn't made in Denmark, it isn't *hygge*.

Given the importance of comfort to the *hygge* lifestyle, it is not surprising that, to the *hygge*-ster, correct under-wear is key. The leading brand in Denmark is Snugpårt®, founded by the revered Olympian Sigge Lauridsen.

(Lauridsen won gold in biathlon in both 1998 and 2002, prompting Queen Margrethe to make him a Companion of the Honourable Order of the Golden Polecat.)

Snugpårt® makes a very wide range of underwear for men, women and children, as well as a number of specialised lines aimed at people with diverse lifestyles.

The breadth of the Snugpårt® range perhaps reflects Sigge Lauridsen himself. Lauridsen revealed in 2004 that he is bisexual, an *årborwånkkerer* and preoccupied by dark sexual fantasies.

(Lauridsen was universally applauded in Denmark for his honesty – which, one hopes, will help normalise other dangerous fetishists.)

Although Lauridsen's high profile surely helps sales, the popularity of Snugpårt® underwear can be attributed to its exceptional comfort. Freja Børnjoka has described the feeling of wearing a Snugpårt® bra as like having her breasts cupped by a giant panda.

Fashion has the potential to deplete *hygge* in environments where it becomes a source of competition. In London or New York, for example, one regularly suspects one's appearance is being judged. Such a feeling is, of course, incompatible with *hygge*.

There is no such problem in Denmark. When I cycle through the icy streets of Aarhus I am never prompted to wonder whether my outfit 'makes the grade'.

That's in part because – as Institute of Wellbeing research has established – most Danes generally spend roughly similar amounts on their wardrobes (around 125,000 kroner, or £15,000, in a typical year).

It may also be because *hygge*-sters wear nearly identical outfits. It is very unusual to find a garment for sale in Denmark in a colour other than black, blue or brown, for example. (Additional colours are sometimes found on knitted jumpers.)

We come now to the controversial matter of slippers. It is fair, I think, to assume that most people around the world consider Denmark the home of soft indoor-only footwear.

Denmark is by far the biggest player in the $120 billion global slipper market. Since the so-called 'Slipper Wars' of the 1990s – which crushed the Canadian slipper industry – Denmark has in fact achieved a near monopoly.

Renewed attempts by the government of Justin Trudeau to force the World Trade Organization to investigate Denmark's slipper business have been greeted with open contempt in Copenhagen.

Speaking on the fringes of the 2016 G20 meeting, where he was part of the EU delegation, our business minister Sejr Twåt was widely assumed to be referring to Mr

Trudeau when he was caught on camera telling an Indian delegate: 'It's going to take more than great hair and running to the WTO like a girl.'

There is one other piece of *hygge* apparel which cannot be ignored when discussing Danish fashion. I write here – of course – of the 'onesie', which was invented in Aalborg by the Snugpårt® Corporation.

In is interesting to note that our Institute of Wellbeing fact-finding team found the onesie to have been widely adopted by the British in Kent and Essex.

We established that many Brits find it convenient to wear such an item because it is appropriate for both the bed and the sofa. (Many Britons shuffle between one and the other for days – even weeks – at a time.)

In Denmark, however, we have progressed far beyond the onesie. Snugpårt® has launched 'twosies', 'three-sies', 'foursies' and even 'fivesies'.

It is not unusual to see a whole Danish family sitting together quietly in one garment. At the Institute of Wellbeing we welcome this trend. Our Flørboscope™ has proven that such behaviour is highly *hygge*.

In 2013 the Danish cinnamon bun (or ruudfynger) was awarded 'European heritage status' and exempted from the EU's Bark Derived Spices Directive Number 8769.

26.

baked goods

Hygge cuisine relies on a range of healthy and flavoursome staples such as cardamom, kelp, juniper, elk, yoghurt, polecat, forest fruits and *årsfish*.

All Danes pay close attention to sourcing food which is local and in season (admittedly, this is made easier by the fact one of our seasons – winter – lasts for much of the year). Where possible, food is foraged.

Foraging is not considered a laughable pretension in Denmark, but a sensible and *hygge*-sure way to find organic protein sources while exercising.

Many readers will be aware of the trendsetting Copenhagen restaurant Misnomer, which exclusively serves foraged foods.

Chef-patron Bent Stetsen and his team scour the intertidal zone every morning at dawn hunting a rich and deli-
cious mix of sea-vegetables, edible birdlife and bottom-
feeding bivalves.

But it is the humble cinnamon bun (or *ruudfynger*) which
is both the most familiar and *hyggeligt* of foodstuffs.
Now, you are perhaps thinking: 'Ah yes, here we are, the
Danish pastry.'

Please stop.

What many around the world call the 'Danish pastry' is
not, in fact, Danish at all. It is an Austrian confection.
Indeed, in Denmark, such pastries are called *wienerbrød*,
or 'Vienna Bread'.

Cinnamon buns, however, are thoroughly Danish – and
thoroughly *hygge*.

You can imagine, then, the seriousness (and frankly fear)
with which Danes greeted the news that the European
Union intended to impose a directive which would
require bakers everywhere – Denmark included – to limit
the amount of cinnamon in their buns on health grounds.

So-called 'Cinnamon-Gate', which rolled on for much of
2013, was considered by many Danes to be nothing less
than an existential threat to the *hygge* way of life. The

directive was seen as more than a matter of national pride. It was seen as a matter of national survival.

There was a widespread clamour to follow our friends in Greenland and leave the EU altogether.

Danes – known for their self-righteous neutrality – were, it seemed, ready to go on the offensive. Riot police were deployed in several urban centres.

The government – fearing further escalation – moved quickly. Within days Denmark had unilaterally applied tariffs to Italian biscotti, Belgian buns and Jaffa Cakes from the United Kingdom.

Amid this rising panic, the EU backed down, and agreement was finally reached on 12 December 2013. Danish cinnamon buns were awarded 'European heritage status' and exempted from the EU's Bark Derived Spices Directive Number 8769.

Though not formally a national holiday, many Danes use some of their generous annual leave entitlement to spend 12 December at home, eating cinnamon buns.

Bun Fun Day shouldn't be confused with that other popular but unofficial celebration Bum Fun Day, which was established by the Olympian and business magnate Sigge Lauridsen, and is usually held on 14 May.

A typical Dane – according to data from Denmark's Obesity Task Force – eats between 11 and 16 cinnamon buns in an average week. This makes Danes the world's second-highest consumers of pastries.

Only the United States consumes more. (The typical American eats some 19 buns or pastries in a normal week.)

Despite my fellow citizens' enthusiasm for buns, however, there is very little obesity in Denmark (unlike the US, of course). In fact, Denmark has by far the lowest rate of obesity in the OECD. The Obesity Task Force voted to disband itself earlier this year, telling reporters it had nothing to do.

So, as you can imagine, when my late colleague Dr Skip King (from Albuquerque University's Department of Comfort Studies) came to Aarhus in 2012, he rather stood out.

Danes are simply not used to meeting such a monumentally obese and wheezing figure as Dr King and many did not know how to behave – which was regrettable and a not a little shaming.

Poor Dr King was laughed at, prodded and asked whether he could touch his own genitals. It was one of the few times in my life that I've been embarrassed by the behaviour of other Danes.

We pride ourselves on tolerance and respect – very much a part of the *hygge* way – but it seems ignorance undermined those values on this occasion.

I'm confident that if another grotesquely fat man was to visit the institute, we would all behave with a little more empathy. (The answer, incidentally, was 'no'.)

A typical Danish family will pay around three months' salary for its collection of Christmas decorations (excluding lights and candles).

27.

taxes

When I attend conferences beyond the Nordic region I am frequently asked about our system of taxation – and, of course, whether it is *hygge*.

This is a question which arises most often in the United Kingdom and the United States, but I have been asked about taxation in Italy, Australia and Nigeria too.

The implicit thought process behind the question is as follows:

Hygge requires a reassuring sense of comfort and immunity from unpleasantness, so surely the constant fear of very large tax demands is undermining of the very *hygge* one seeks to locate?

This is deeply flawed thinking. Indeed, it is almost the inverse of the truth. Given the regularity with which I am asked about taxation, then, I feel it is important to take a brief moment to explain how high taxes, in fact, are the very bedrock of the *hygge* society.

First let me briefly describe how taxation works in Denmark.

Our income tax rate varies from 47 per cent on earnings up to 60,000 kroner per annum (roughly £7,000) all the way up to 100 per cent on earnings over 500,000 kroner per annum (around £55,000). There are 26 tax bands between those two thresholds.

Taxes such as VAT and other duties are applied to all products, services and activities in Denmark.

The biggest revenue raisers, however, are the flat taxes imposed on the manufacturing of candles, candle purchases, the lighting of candles, the extinguishing of candles and – of course – the disposal of candles.

If you are reading this book in a so-called 'Anglo-Saxon' capitalist economy (such as the UK or the US) you will no doubt regard the high level of taxation in Denmark with horror. But, if so, you are wrong to do so.

High taxes create *hygge* and there are two clear reasons why that is so.

The first and most obvious is that, far from making individuals feel vulnerable, very high tax demands allow our government to maintain an economy which protects everyone.

There are no losers here. That sense of safety – and the equalising effect of our massively redistributive tax system – means that there is almost no hierarchy in Denmark, and certainly no 'class system'. The equality and peace-of-mind found in such a society is fundamentally *hygge*.

The sad truth – and I'm afraid there is no way to cinnamon-coat this – is that non-Danish readers might well be able to nudge their lives in a *hyggeligt* direction, and I encourage everyone to try, but they will never achieve a fully *hygge* lifestyle in a society less perfectly balanced than Denmark's.

(Which, of course, is every other society on earth.)

The other reason why *hygge*-sters positively love paying tax is that they know they are directly and personally contributing to the creation of this Danish *hygge*-topia.

Danes do not worry that they might be paying their taxes while their neighbour or boss is not. Everyone is paying!

It is one of our favourite things to do. The idea that a Dane would avoid or evade tax is simply ludicrous.

Speaking personally, I delight in paying tax. Doing so makes me feel keenly *hygge*. I simply imagine the sort of people my hard-won money is supporting.

I think of all those parents of young children who surely need their 78 months paid parental leave.

I imagine retirees who, after working hard for 24 long years, have unquestionably earned the right to a financially secure rest. Good luck to them, I think. Enjoy!

One should not be surprised, then, that our indefatigable political leaders regularly invent innovative new ways to tax the ever-willing Danish worker.

Earlier this month, for example, a bill reached our parliament which would see every Dane of working age (25–49) issued with an 'activity tracker'.

Data would be sent automatically to the Inland Revenue which would then bill citizens monthly according to how many steps they had taken.

The higher the step-count, the higher the bill.

This revenue stream would be 'hypothecated', meaning it would be reserved solely for the upkeep of pavements.

The reaction in Denmark to this idea has so far been characteristically positive.

There has only ever been one 'tax revolt' in Denmark. It erupted in 2009 when the then Social Democrat–Democratic Socialist–Progressive coalition government announced plans to impose a modest 4 per cent tax increase on internet pornography.

The idea was a political own-goal and quickly abandoned.

That incident aside, however, there have been very few figures in Danish political history who question our approach to fiscal policy.

The highest profile of those who do so today, of course, is Tad Klåknuter (leader of the right-wing Denmark's Bosom party).

Klåknuter argued in a speech in 2015 that our high level of taxation might be contributing to Denmark's relatively low productivity.

As you can imagine, Klåknuter's remarks were met with open derision. There were raucous shouts of 'Arthur Laffer was misguided' and 'the trickle-down effect is probably an illusion'.

It's not often that I feel sympathy for Tad Klåknuter (whose politics are, needless to say, very different from mine), but I did that evening. No one likes to see the spectacle of a man – any man – have to face down such undignified barracking.

28.

animals

There is one question I am asked almost daily by someone, somewhere in the world. Dr Olsensen, they write, are pets *hygge*?

The answer, of course, is yes.

These days, I pre-empt the inevitable follow-up question. 'And the pet you should have,' I write, 'is a dog'.

I am aware, of course, that this is controversial. Even within the relatively closed world of well-being and happiness studies, there are widely divergent views on this subject.

I will take a moment here to explain my advice.

At the Institute of Wellbeing in Aarhus we have used our Flørboscope™ technology to measure *hygge*-ness in a very wide range of animals

– not just common pets but some wild animals too, including the polecat and the bear.

At this point in my lectures I am almost always asked whether any animals were harmed during our research with the Flørboscope™. The answer is yes.

At the Institute of Wellbeing we stand by our research, however, and consider the question settled. The dog is – by some considerable margin – the most *hygge* domestic animal available.

(The polecat is the most *hygge* wild animal – according to our data – but experience suggests they are not recommendable as pets.)

The canine reliably meets the basic requirements one looks for in a *hygge* animal: they pad along behind you contentedly, and sit with you on demand.

As a general rule, shorter-haired dogs are likely to be more *hygge*-friendly than long-haired breeds, simply because they get very cold in the frigid Danish climate and will require more warming and (from the human point of view) *hygge*-inducing contact.

My own dog, Shlløng (Danish for 'little monkey') – a beautiful Chinese crested hound – is a very good example. He frequently jumps onto my lap, his tiny wrinkled body shivering uncontrollably.

It is easy to see how the presence of a small hairless dog helps to foster *hygge* at home. But do consider taking your pet to the workplace too. My colleagues at the Institute of Wellbeing always seem pleased to see my quivering little Shlløng.

We should take a moment to consider the Great Dane. Great Danes are wonderful animals and very *hygge*; short-haired and pleasingly affectionate, despite their equine proportions.

Interestingly, Great Danes were known as Store Norsks (Big Norwegians) until 1035 when Cnut the Great, son of Forkbeard, lost his mind shortly before his death and abdicated in favour of his Store Norsk, Cnut the Hairy.

Hairy Cnut, as he was known in the royal court, technically ruled over Denmark for 48 uneventful minutes before a violent coup was mounted by furious noblemen.

The former king was decapitated and Hairy Cnut was tricked into abandoning the throne by a coup-leader who threw a stick out of the window. Store Norsks have been known as Great Danes ever since that turbulent day (which also gave Denmark the colloquialism 'acting like a mad cnut').

It is not possible to say that cats are *hygge* simply because there is such wide variation between individuals.

Some cats are exceedingly *hygge*, as our Flørboscope™ has shown. They can be warmly affectionate and pleasingly aesthetic. Purring is compatible with *hygge* (unlike barking). But many cats are selfish, anti-social and aggressive. Sharing your home with such an animal will quickly erode *hygge*.

My own experience with cats makes the point. Before that happy day in 2011 when I came face to face with Shlløng for the first time, I had 'adopted' six mewling kittens – one after another – from the Aarhus Animal Rescue Centre. Each time I had had to return the animal, having found it to be *unhygge*.

I'm sure they have all been rehomed now, or perhaps humanely destroyed. Either way, it's best not to dwell on it. (Being *hygge*, after all, means living in the moment.)

Many Danes, of course, seek to get close to wildlife. This certainly can be a *hygge* thing to do, not least because it provides an opportunity to enjoy Denmark's wild spaces (see pages 63). For most *hygge*-sters, the greatest prize is to get alongside a polecat (or *mustela putorius*).

One doesn't really need a Flørboscope™ to know that polecats are *hygge*. Small, curious and adorably furry, polecats mark their territory by secreting a foul-smelling fluid from their anuses.

It will perhaps be of some surprise to Britons to note that the cultural representation of the polecat there and in Denmark has long been markedly – and interestingly – different.

In the United Kingdom polecats are viewed with disgust for their wanton promiscuity. (The polecat is indeed energetically polygamous.)

London prostitutes are often called 'polecats' and the association stretches back at least as far as the days of Shakespeare. (*The Merry Wives of Windsor*, for example, includes the line 'Out of my door, you witch, you hag, you baggage, you polecat, you runyon!')

Denmark, however, views the polecat rather differently. Here it is a compliment to be described as a 'polecat', and many Danish women aspire to be considered one. Admiring polecat references in Danish literature can be found from at least the Middle Ages.

Since the Nordic polecat is no less obviously promiscuous than its British cousin, we might assume that the different connotations reflect differences in sexual attitudes between the two nations.

This is not a new observation. Scholars today generally accept that this was exactly what Shakespeare had in mind when he declared there to be 'something rotten in the state of Denmark'.

29.

funfairs

I have been asked by my publisher to include a short chapter on funfairs simply because they are widely – but incorrectly – assumed to be *hygge* by people who are new to the lifestyle.

Funfairs are not *hygge*. The clue is in the name. They are not comfortfairs, or cosyfairs or even *hygge*fairs. The problem, I'm afraid, is what constitutes 'fun'.

I accept, of course, that so-called 'funfairs' can – superficially at least – appear *hygge*, particularly at night. Warm lights, whimsical music and sugary treats can indeed create a pleasing atmosphere. The sound of families laughing excitedly is not, I concede, disagreeable.

There is even a familiar funfair attraction which is, taken in isolation, *hygge*: the Ferris wheel.

One can find much to admire about the Ferris wheel. (It is no coincidence that Mr Ferris was a respected Danish engineer and something of a mentor to the young Agnes Agnessen.)

The wheel's narrow seating is usefully *hygge*, pressing companions together, and the machine itself rotates slowly and gently enough for its occupants to both enjoy the views and consume warm beverages and cinnamon buns packed for the occasion.

Recalling my own childhood in Aarhus, I enjoyed some wonderfully *hygge* moments on Ferris wheels – particularly those occasions when the wheel stopped to board new riders, leaving my dear mother and I suspended in the cool evening gale.

I remember the warmth I felt as I waved happily to children from my school, waiting in the queue below. They, in turn, smiled up at us – pointing and laughing.

But, make no mistake, there is little else at the funfair that could possibly be described as *hygge*.

Other rides play on people's primal fear of speed and disorientation. The music – which from a distance appeared whimsical – turns out, on closer hearing, to be unlistenable Europop. The couples one saw laughing wildly next the waltzer turn out to be vomiting over their own shoes.

More threateningly, the funfair workers – who one might imagine to be boyishly simple but kindly folk – turn out to be scarred and intimidating thugs, trying every trick they can think of to relieve you of your kroner (and your daughters of their virginity).

The coconut shy, rifle range, hook-a-duck and test-of-strength games are all a fix. You cannot win. And if by some fluke you do, there's a realistic chance you will be followed home by the grizzled stallholder and killed.

No, the funfair is not fun – and certainly not *hygge*. And I haven't even described the least *hygge* so-called 'attraction' of them all: bumper cars.

The premise is appealing enough. Children and adults are each given a small electric (and hence zero-carbon) car and invited to drive them alongside one another in wide circles.

You would think all drivers would pursue a broadly similar loop, to avoid accident, and that the operator would quickly shut off the power in the event of any collision.

You would be wrong.

When in 1979 I climbed into a bumper car (for the first and only time) at a funfair in the Lisbjerg suburb of Aarhus, I immediately sensed that I might have miscalculated.

The sticky faux-leather seats, dangerously loose steering wheel and inadequate seat-belts told me that – at the very least – I had found myself in an unsafe vehicle. But that was far from the worst of it.

When the buzzer sounded, indicating that the power was flowing (though I did not realise that, and remained stationary), my fellow drivers – many of them Norwegian teenagers on a coach tour of Denmark – began to ram my flimsy machine from every conceivable angle.

It was an appallingly violent, savage and *unhygge* episode which upset me greatly at the time (and even today still saddens me).

But as I sat there, tears rolling down my cheeks, enduring the constant bone-shaking slams of other cars into mine, I resolved to chart a course in life which would never again expose me to such conflict.

That course led me, eventually, to the Institute of Wellbeing. In some ways, perhaps, I have those out-of-control Norwegian teenagers to thank for the way my life has unfolded so agreeably.

poetry

After profoundly dark television serials (see page 75) poetry is, to the *hygge*-ster, the most complete art form.

Hyggeligt individuals (and here I include myself) not only read poetry late into the night, but write it too.

The quietly cosy appeal of verse is perfectly obvious, and here in Denmark we are blessed with a remarkably rich canon.

The names of ancient poets reverberate down the generations: Furrhøle the Bold, Skåt of Gorm and Kråkk Hørr. These are poets whose works remain familiar to every Dane, many centuries after they were written.

Our modern poets, too, are globally recognised for the quality and pioneering spirit of their balladry.

Poets such as Års Tråpp, Rud Spunkling and – of course – our current poet laureate Børl Bågg, are all *hus*-hold names here in Denmark.

They have achieved a level of recognition and respect reserved, in other cultures, for star footballers or popular musicians.

While it is delightfully *hygge* to attempt to decode the complex syntax of these masters while bathed in low light, even greater levels of *hygge* can be achieved through the composition of one's own original verse.

There is nothing – nothing – that restores me like a weekend spent in our isolated family cabin, alone, silently forming couplets, with Terje Dørk on the turnta-ble and my little Shlløng curled up in my lap.

For some Danes, poetry is a shared experience.

The rise of *poesitræerslams* (roughly: 'poet-tree-slams') – group spoken word sessions held in woodland loca-tions by candlelight – have become hugely popular here, particularly among groups of men.

They use verse – much of it spontaneous – to articulate powerful truths about what it means to be a Danish male today.

Some view these sessions with a degree of suspicion, imagining the poetry to be nothing but a convenient cover story – masking less savoury pursuits.

And, in fairness, I have attended *poesitræerslams* which have descended into bouts of fierce *årborwånkkering* (and even, on one occasion, prolonged same-sex *ånuscandling*).

But, in general, *poesitræerslams* should be taken at face value, and encouraged. We now understand a great deal more about the fragile mental health of men throughout the post-industrial world.

It would be wrong, in light of that knowledge, to discourage any shared bonding experience – particularly those held in a woodland setting – however depraved un*hygge*lightened people might consider the chosen group activity to be.

Although I tend to compose poetry only for my own personal development, I have been encouraged to share one of my recent works here – somewhat against my better judgement, I have to say – in the hope it provides a useful example.

Please forgive the lack of sophistication in this work. I am under no illusions: I am no Børl Bågg.

It is entitled, simply, 'Freja'. I hope you enjoy it.

The light meter
did not
defeat her
Now she coils
Slippery
in essential oils
Eyes wide
A storm outside
Her cosy place
Her candlelit face
Waiting
For gørhorn

31.
denmark

In this short but hopefully useful volume, I have attempted to explain *hygge*. In doing so, however, I have just as often found myself writing of Denmark and its traditions.

That's because *hygge* and Denmark are thoroughly interwoven. But I fear that in describing Denmark only as the canvas on which *hygge* is painted, I may have offered an incomplete picture.

So, with the few lines remaining, I would like to share some facts about my country.

We are the least corrupt nation in the world, according to Transparency International, and the happiest, according to research commissioned by the United Nations.

We have very high social mobility (a poor Danish child is twice as likely as a poor child in the United States to join the top fifth of earners in their lifetime), and a very low crime rate.

We have high per capita income enjoyed by those at the top, and a generous welfare system catching those at the bottom.

We have a rich cultural heritage, a long tradition of dark good humour, pristine wild spaces, sophisticated urban centres – and a population smaller than London's to share it all.

And, of course, we have *hygge*.

No one in Denmark would seriously claim our nation to be perfect. But we are at least trying. I hope you will visit Denmark in pursuit of the *hyggeligt* lifestyle, and see for yourself.

acknowledgements

I am grateful to Hannah Black, Emma Knight, Liz Caraffi and their colleagues at Hodder & Stoughton for encouraging me to bring the work of the Institute of Wellbeing to a wider audience.

I'm delighted that, as a result of our collaboration, Hodder & Stoughton itself has decided to apply the *hygge* approach to every area of its business. I look forward to visiting you in your new *køntorgling* office space.

My colleagues at the Institute of Wellbeing in Aarhus have been immensely supportive. In particular I would like to thank: Aksel Forstårsen, Sophia Nordskov, Jesper Jensen, Agata Pedersen, Emmelie Eriksson and Olaf Flåp.

The study of wellbeing is a wonderfully collaborative field and I'm grateful to researchers at several other organisations for helping to me to understand their research, and allowing me to quote from it.

Special thanks to Dr Karl Karlsson, for pointing me to his excellent paper in *Annals of Swedish Unhappiness*.

Professor Olaf Poång, our founder, has been a source of inspiration and wise council to me for many years now. Olaf: I hope you feel I have done our discipline a service in writing this book. I look forward to discussing it with you soon in a friendly jurisdiction.

Freja Børnjoka has been an indispensable help to me over the last year, as I have juggled commitments to the institute with writing this book and divorcing my wife. Freja: you have taught me ways to feel *hygge* that I did not know and frankly could not have imagined.

Finally, I wish to thank two dear and *hyggeligt* friends: Keith Moore, for his wonderful contributions to this book; and especially Richard Knight, for helping me to find my voice in English.

glossary

ålgørithm – a set of instructions written in code for the purposes of programming Danish-only software

ånuscandling – a sometimes eye-watering sexual practice popular in the Syddanmark region and a sub-genre of *candlepørn*

årborwånkkering – the Danish practice of masturbating quietly in a forest setting

årsfish – an abundant white fish with a distinctive aroma found off the coast of Denmark, and a staple of *hygge* cuisine

Bållswårm® – leading brand of fleece micro-blankets, often used in *hyggesacs*

bløofunkt – an inexplicable gnawing feeling of despair which can overcome some Danes despite being the World's Happiest People™

Bønår – iconic *hygge* villa, designed by the architect Agnes Agnessen, which famously collapsed in 2006

candlepørn – generic name for candle-related pornography, widely consumed in Denmark, which includes subgenres *ånuscandling* and *høtwåxing*

drøn jazz – a uniquely Danish style of jazz featuring bleak jarring chord sequences played on non-standard jazz instruments such as the bassoon and oboe

dymglåss – widely used style of Danish glazing designed to achieve the optimal level of interior gloom, particularly in *køntorgling* offices

En Retfærdig Straf – hugely popular and genre-defining Danish film depicting the life of a sensitive medieval executioner

ffåd – a short-lived and insubstantial gimmick

flåymshafts – candles ('candles' is also widely used)

flåymshaftsplus – very bright candles ('very bright candles' is also widely used)

fløggriders – traditional Danish trouser made from hessian and polecat fur, worn by both men and women on Christmas morn

Flørboscope™ – patented Institute of Wellbeing instrument used for measuring *hygge*

flyggpigscråper – revolutionary Danish agricultural machine used for making bacon

føkking – the process of making one's garden unpleasant

Folketinget – Denmark's unicameral national parliament

frørdes – the unproven 'third circle of *hygge*', the highest state of *hygge*lightenment thought by some to have been achieved by a handful of people for a fleeting moment (see *ønnsåfrabble*)

gløgg – warm spice-infused beverage with a red wine base

gørhorn – state of sexual readiness combining deep relaxation with advanced tumescence

hej dikwåd – popular traditional Danish game played outdoors, rules vary widely by region

høtwaxing – a generally pleasing sexual practice popular in the Sjælland region and a sub-genre of *candlepørn*

Hippenflåsk – narrow drinking vessel, often with polecat leather trim, traditionally used to carry strong *gløgg* to sporting fixtures

Hyggeadvisor – app directing users to *hygge*-friendly destinations, restaurants and hotels worldwide

Hyggebrikførskkin – defining text on *hygge* architecture by Agnes Agnessen, published in 1979

hyggeligt – very *hygge* or having the characteristics of *hygge*

Hyggelightened/hyggelightenment – a state of perfect *hygge*xistance passed into by one who acquires pure *hygge* wisdom (used informally to describe people sympathetic to the *hygge* lifestyle)

hyggesac – small bag used for carrying *hygge* essentials, particularly on longer journeys

Ja! Ja! Ja! – traditional outdoor game based on ancient Norse fertility rituals

Jåp's Eye – defining *drøn* jazz album released by Mads Jåp in 1981 on the Bøtfunk label

'Jøksplåt, Jesu, Jøksplåt' – traditional Christmas carol sung by most Danes, religious or secular, after the lighting of the tree

Jul – Christmas (celebrated, in Denmark, on 24 December)

Jyslåmp – iconic lamp with two settings designed by the leading Danish designer Malthe Hvorsen

Køksokk –Danish tent and camping equipment manufacturer with headquarters in Roskilde

køntorgling – holistic *hygge*-friendly office design philosophy pioneered by Marcus Gonåddsen in the 1960s

lyslyters – workers employed to light and extinguish candles

måndskylkke – a vulgar Danish insult combining connotations of extreme miserliness and inappropriate sexual interest in polecats

Nu-Agnessen School – contemporary architects working in the tradition of Agnes Agnessen, the famous proponent of *hygge* design

ønnsåfrabble – the unproven so-called 'second circle of *hygge*', the second-highest state of *hygge*lightenment (see *frørdes*)

PassivAggressivHaus – stringent Danish sustainable design standard based on but superior to the PassivHaus certification

poesitræerslams – literally 'poet-tree-slams', group spoken word poetry events held in forests

rumbumfårtling – snow-shoeing

rumbumfårtlingfeber – 'snow-shoeing fever', usually a reference to increased enthusiasm for snow-shoeing following the 1980 Winter Olympics in which Denmark triumphed in the discipline

runfart – traditional Danish outdoor game for 6-8 players requiring bats, shuttlecocks, darts and spoons

ruudfynger – cinnamon-flavoured bread or pastry, widely popular in Denmark

shåttstørmer – sudden and explosive defecation due to ill-health or food-poisoning

sokbøld – widely played indoor game in which rolled socks are bowled underarm

Snugpårt® – Denmark's leading brand of undergarments founded by Olympic champion Sigge Lauridsen

tøtålkunst – taking pleasure in another's misfortune, similar to the German *schadenfreude*

unhygge – someone or something which is not *hygge*

untfårrågehøle – one who lacks empathy or basic human decency

Unturdførb – aesthetically pleasing toilet brush designed by Malthe Hvorsen in 1926, which is still a significant Danish export

An invitation from the publisher

Join us at www.hodder.co.uk, or follow us
on Twitter @hodderbooks to be a part of
our community of people who love the very
best in books and reading.

Whether you want to discover more about a book
or an author, watch trailers and interviews, have the
chance to win early limited editions, or simply browse
our expert readers' selection of the very best books,
we think you'll find what you're looking for.

And if you don't, that's the place to tell us what's missing.

We love what we do, and we'd love you to be a part of it.

www.hodder.co.uk

@hodderbooks

HodderBooks

HodderBooks